Money Mastery for Young Adults Made Easy

YOUR 8-STEP GUIDE TO ACHIEVE FINANCIAL CONFIDENCE, REDUCE DEBT, INVEST WISELY, AND SET LONG-TERM FINANCIAL GOALS

RON MARTIN, CPA

© Copyright RON MARTIN CPA 2024 - **All rights reserved.**

The content within this book may not be reproduced, duplicated or transmitted without direct written permission from the author or the publisher.

Under no circumstances will any blame or legal responsibility be held against the publisher, or author, for any damages, reparation, or monetary loss due to the information contained within this book. Either directly or indirectly. You are responsible for your own choices, actions, and results.

Legal Notice:

This book is copyright protected. This book is only for personal use. You cannot amend, distribute, sell, use, quote or paraphrase any part, of the content within this book, without the consent of the author or publisher.

Disclaimer Notice:

Please note the information contained within this document is for educational and entertainment purposes only. All effort has been expended to present accurate, up-to-date, and reliable, complete information. No warranties of any kind are declared or implied. Readers acknowledge that the author is not engaging in the rendering of legal, financial, medical or professional advice. The content within this book has been derived from various sources. Please consult a licensed professional before attempting any techniques outlined in this book.

By reading this document, the reader agrees that under no circumstances is the author responsible for any losses, direct or indirect, which are incurred as a result of the use of the information contained within this document, including, but not limited to, — errors, omissions, or inaccuracies.

TABLE OF CONTENTS

Introduction   7

1. LAYING THE FINANCIAL FOUNDATIONS   11
   1.1 Crafting Your First Budget: A Step-by-Step Guide   12
   1.2 The Basics of Saving: Techniques That Work   15
   1.3 Essential Banking Know-How for Beginners   18
   1.4 Setting Up Your Financial Toolkit: Apps and Platforms   20
   1.5 Decoding Financial Jargon: Simplifying Complex Terms   22

2. MASTERING CASH FLOW AND DEBT MANAGEMENT   25
   2.1 Strategies for Living Beyond Paycheck to Paycheck   26
   2.2 Smart Debt Handling: Credit Cards and Student Loans   28
   2.3 Negotiating Better Terms on Existing Debts   30
   2.4 Innovative Ways to Increase Your Income   32
   2.5 Managing Recurring Payments and Subscriptions   34
   2.6 Emergency Funds: How Much and How Soon   36

3. INVESTING AND GROWING YOUR WEALTH   39
   3.1 Stocks and Bonds: Investing 101 for Beginners   40
   3.2 Retirement Accounts: Starting in Your 20s   42
   3.3 Real Estate as an Investment: What You Need to Know   44
   3.4 Ethical and Impact Investing for a Better World   47
   3.5 Common Investing Mistakes and How to Avoid Them   50
   3.6 Using Tech Tools for Smarter Investing   52

4. NAVIGATING LIFE CHANGES AND FINANCIAL
   DECISIONS   55
   4.1 Financial Planning for College Students   56
   4.2 Handling Finances After Graduation: What's
       Next?   58
   4.3 Financial Considerations for New Couples   60
   4.4 Planning for Financial Emergencies   62
   4.5 Job Loss: Managing Finances During
       Unemployment   64
   4.6 Relocating: Budgeting for a Big Move   67

5. ADVANCED BUDGETING AND SAVING
   STRATEGIES   73
   5.1 Zero-Based vs. 50/30/20 Budgeting Models   74
   5.2 Automating Your Savings: Set It and Forget It   76
   5.3 Hack Your Savings: Tips for Bigger Growth   78
   5.4 Seasonal Budget Adjustments: Planning for
       Holidays and Vacations   81
   5.5 Couponing and Discount Shopping in the
       Digital Age   83
   5.6 Side Hustles: Balancing Time and Money   85

6. CREDIT MASTERY AND AVOIDING PITFALLS   89
   6.1 Building Your Credit from Scratch   90
   6.2 Repairing Bad Credit: A Recoverable Journey   92
   6.3 Understanding and Using Credit Wisely   95
   6.4 Credit Myths Debunked   97
   6.5 Protecting Yourself Against Credit Fraud   99
   6.6 Credit and Major Purchases: What to Know   101

7. TAX ESSENTIALS AND MAXIMIZING YOUR
   INCOME   105
   7.1 Basics of Taxes for Young Adults   106
   7.2 Tax Deductions and Credits: What You Can
       Claim   108
   7.3 Freelancing and Taxes: Keeping It Straight   110
   7.4 Investment Taxes: What You Need to Know   113
   7.5 Salary Negotiation Tactics for Your First Job   116
   7.6 Passive Income: Making Money While You
       Sleep   118

8. BUILDING FINANCIAL INDEPENDENCE AND
   SECURITY   121
   8.1 Financial Milestones for Your 20s and 30s   122
   8.2 Long-Term Financial Planning: Looking Ahead   124
   8.3 Insurance: Types, Needs, and Decisions   126
   8.4 Estate Planning Basics for Young Adults   129
   8.5 Achieving Financial Freedom: Real Stories,
       Real Advice   131
   8.6 Keeping Up with Financial Trends: Staying
       Informed   134

   Summarizing Financial Savvy   137
   References   139

INTRODUCTION

Have you ever felt like you're just spinning your wheels, trying to get a grip on your finances? You're not alone. Many young adults find themselves in a maze of credit scores, budgeting dilemmas, and significant financial decisions, often needing a clear guide on what to do next. But what if you could change that narrative? What if you could step into a world where managing your money felt possible and enjoyable?

Hi, I'm Ron Martin, a retired Certified Public Accountant (CPA) whose passion now is to guide young adults like you through the often intimidating world of personal finance. Having navigated these waters successfully with my children, I've seen firsthand the challenges and triumphs of reaching financial independence. I bring to you the expertise from my professional life and real, lived experiences and successes that can help light your path.

"Money Mastery for Young Adults Made Easy: Your 8-Step Guide to Achieve Financial Confidence, Reduce Debt, Invest Wisely, and

Set Long-term Financial Goals" is crafted with a clear mission: to arm you with a step-by-step blueprint for financial empowerment. This book breaks from the traditional, stodgy financial guides by embracing current technology to make learning about finances engaging and actionable.

Imagine starting a journey where each step enhances your confidence and control over your money. That's what I promise here—a shift from confusion to clarity in handling your finances. This book teaches you the fundamentals of personal finance and how to apply these principles tailored to your unique lifestyle and goals.

The importance of being financially literate must be balanced, especially in today's economy. Statistics show that young adults who grasp the essentials of personal finance early in life are better equipped to avoid common financial pitfalls like overwhelming debt and poor savings habits. This book is designed to set you on a better path, filled with informed decisions that pave the way for long-term stability and success.

I understand the skepticism—another book on personal finance? What makes this one different? Here's my commitment to you: no fluff, just practical, actionable advice based on real-world scenarios and tested strategies. I'm here to share what works, not just theories and concepts.

In the following pages, you'll find a detailed breakdown of topics ranging from budgeting and saving to investing. Each chapter builds on the last, creating a comprehensive guide to refer to at different stages of your financial journey.

So, let's get started. Dive into this playbook with an open mind and a willingness to tackle your financial challenges head-on. Here's to maximizing your financial potential and transforming how you interact with money. I encourage you to take notes, ask questions, and, most importantly, share your successes as you move forward. You can email me at martinrondec@gmail.com. Together, let's take control of your financial future!

CHAPTER 1
LAYING THE FINANCIAL FOUNDATIONS

So, you've just landed your first real job, or maybe you're wrestling with the beast of student loan debt, wondering how to save for a future home, a dream vacation, or just next week's groceries. If the thought of looking at your bank account gives you more anxiety than watching a horror movie alone at night, then you're in the right place. Welcome to the no-judgment zone where we tackle the first giant monster under the bed: budgeting.

Yes, budgeting. It's not just something your penny-pinching Aunt Bertha raves about at family reunions. The secret weapon can transform your financial chaos into a well-oiled machine. Now, before you roll your eyes and mumble, "Easier said than done," let me walk you through this. We're not just going to talk about budgeting —we're going to break it down into bite-sized pieces so quickly that even your dog could do it (if he had thumbs and a little cash).

1.1 CRAFTING YOUR FIRST BUDGET: A STEP-BY-STEP GUIDE

What's a Budget and Why Should You Care?

First off, let's demystify this whole budget thing. A budget is simply a plan for your money. It's knowing how much you earn versus how much you spend and ensuring the latter never exceeds the former. But it's more than just numbers and spreadsheets—it's about taking control. It's about ensuring you have enough for pizza nights and pesky unexpected bills. It's about empowerment —steering the ship of your financial life instead of drifting aimlessly.

The Nitty-Gritty: Setting Up Your Budget

Let's roll up our sleeves and set up your budget. First, you can quickly grab a tool to track your income and expenses. If you're feeling retro, this could be a simple spreadsheet, a budgeting app, or even a good old-fashioned notebook.

1. **List Your Income Sources:** Write down how much money you bring in monthly from all sources—your job, side gigs,

that Etsy shop you run, and yes, even the cash grandma slips you on birthdays.
2. **Track Your Expenses:** Next, jot down all your expenses. And I mean all—from rent and utilities to that morning coffee habit. Divide them into fixed expenses (like rent and car payments) and variable expenses (like groceries and entertainment).
3. **Set Financial Goals:** What are you budgeting for? It could be paying off debt, saving up for a concert, or building an emergency fund. Having clear goals will keep you focused and motivated.
4. **Adjust as Needed:** The first draft of your budget will be challenging. Track your monthly spending, see where you overspend, and adjust. Rinse and repeat until your budget fits you like that favorite pair of jeans.

Exploring Different Budgeting Methods

Not all budgets are equal; the best method depends on your style and financial goals. Let's look at a few popular ones:

- **The Envelope System:** This is old school but effective. Divide your cash for the month into envelopes allocated for different spending categories. Once an envelope is empty, you can no longer spend in that category until next month.
- **Zero-Based Budgeting:** In this method, every dollar gets a job. You allocate every penny you earn to specific expenses, savings, and investments until you have zero dollars "unassigned." It's excellent for meticulous planners.
- **The 50/30/20 Rule:** This is a bit more flexible. Allocate 50% of your income to needs (rent, utilities, groceries), 30% to wants (dining out, hobbies), and 20% to savings

and debt repayment. It's straightforward and easy to remember.

Real-Life Budgeting Wins

Let's ground this in reality with some case studies. Take Clara, a recent grad who used zero-based budgeting to manage her finances and pay off her student loans within two years. Or Mark, who swears by the envelope system to curb impulse buys and save up for his dream gaming setup. These stories aren't just inspiring—they show that budgeting works when you find the method that fits your life.

Budgeting Worksheet

To kickstart your budget-making process, here's a simple worksheet you can set up in Excel or Google Sheets to help you organize your income and expenses. Feel free to customize it to suit your financial situation and goals better.

Income Sources:

- Salary:
- Side gigs:
- Miscellaneous:

Fixed Expenses:

- Rent/Mortgage:
- Utilities:
- Insurance:

Variable Expenses:

- Groceries:
- Dining Out:
- Entertainment:

Financial Goals:

- Short-term (e.g., concert tickets):
- Medium-term (e.g., vacation):
- Long-term (e.g., down payment on a house):

Use this worksheet as a starting point. Adjust the categories and amounts as you track your spending and get a clearer picture of where your money is going. Remember, the goal is to make your budget work for you, not vice versa. So, please take what you need, tweak it, and start taking control of your financial future today!

Now if you are working at your first job, you may not have enough left over to pay for concert tickets. You should sacrifice by choosing free events, like visiting the park or a museum. This is only temporary until you start making more money.

1.2 THE BASICS OF SAVING: TECHNIQUES THAT WORK

Let's talk about saving money, and no, not in the way where you stash every penny under your mattress and live off ramen noodles (unless you really love ramen, then more power to you). Saving is all about setting yourself up for financial success, both now and in the future. It's like building a safety net that grows bigger every time you add to it. Think of it as paying your future self for all your hard work today.

One of the golden rules of saving is "paying yourself first." It's a simple but powerful concept: before you pay your bills, buy groceries, or spend money on entertainment, you set aside a portion of your income for your savings. It's treating your savings account like another bill that must be paid, ensuring that saving money becomes a regular part of your monthly budget. This approach shifts your mindset from saving what is left over at the end of the month (which, let's be honest, might be nothing) to making saving a priority.

How can you make this process as painless as possible? Let's dive into some practical saving techniques that won't feel like a chore. First up, automated transfers. This is a game-changer. Setting up an automatic transfer from your checking account to your savings account each payday means you don't have to think about it—it just happens. Whether it's $50, $100, or even $500, automating this process makes saving effortless. You can set it, forget it, and watch your savings grow without lifting another finger. So that you're not tempted to spend your hard-earned savings, transfer these funds to an online savings account that pays a higher interest rate than your bank (which is usually pretty low). Out of sight, out of mind.

Another nifty way to boost your savings without feeling the pinch is using apps that round up your transactions. Imagine buying a coffee for $3.75; these apps can round up the cost to $4.00 and put that extra $0.25 into your savings. It might not seem like much, but these small amounts can add up surprisingly fast. Before you know it, you've saved enough for a concert ticket or a weekend getaway from the spare change from your daily purchases. One such app is Chime®. With Round-Ups, Chime automatically rounds up purchases made with your Chime debit card to the nearest dollar and transfers the difference from your spending account into your savings account. Alternatively, you can open a bank account at

Bank of America and use their Keep the Change ® Savings Program.

Setting saving goals is another crucial step. Without a goal, saving money can feel like an endless chore. Start by defining what you're saving for. Is it an emergency fund that covers six months of living expenses? A down payment for a new car? Or maybe you're dreaming big and saving for a down payment on a house. Make your goals specific, measurable, achievable, relevant, and time-bound (SMART). This clarity will keep you motivated and help you track your progress and stay committed to your savings plan.

Let's throw in some real-life magic here. Consider the story of Emily, who started her savings journey with nothing but a small paycheck and a big dream to travel Europe. She slowly but steadily built her travel fund by setting a clear goal (one year to save $3,000), using automated transfers, and a round-up app. By the end of the year, not only had she saved enough for her trip, but she also had a little extra to splurge on gelato in Italy. Emily's story isn't just about her enjoying picturesque sunsets in Europe—it's about the power of consistent saving habits and the doors they can open.

So, as you can see, saving isn't just about stashing cash away. It's about creating opportunities for yourself and ensuring a stable, secure financial future. Whether you're just starting or looking to boost your current savings strategy, these techniques are your tools to help build that financial safety net. Remember, every little bit adds up, and the sooner you start, the better off you'll be. So why wait? Get started today, and make saving a habit and a successful part of your financial plan.

1.3 ESSENTIAL BANKING KNOW-HOW FOR BEGINNERS

Let's talk banks. You might think, "Hey, it's just a place to stash my cash, right?" Yes, but there's more to it if you want to manage your money like a pro. Understanding basic banking operations is like knowing how to change a tire—it's not the most thrilling skill, but it's super handy when you need it. Whether you're setting up your first bank account or trying to figure out which banking options will best suit your jet-set lifestyle, I've got the lowdown on everything you need to get started.

First, could you break down the typical accounts at most banks or credit unions? You've got your checking and savings accounts; these are your bread and butter. A checking account is like your everyday wallet—you'll deposit your paycheck, pay bills, and use your debit card for those daily coffee runs. Meanwhile, a savings account is where you stash cash for future goals or emergencies—it's like a piggy bank but with interest. Speaking of interest, it's usually higher in savings accounts, giving you a little extra to keep your money there.

Then there are CDs or certificates of deposit, which are like time capsules for your cash. You agree to lock up your money for a fixed period, and in return, you get a higher interest rate than a regular savings account. It's perfect if you know you won't need to access your funds for a while and want to earn more interest. And let's not forget about money market accounts, which are a bit like hybrids of checking and savings accounts. They offer higher interest rates; you can usually write checks or use a debit card directly from the account.

Now, choosing where to bank is as crucial as choosing a decent coffee shop. You wouldn't go to a place that serves burnt espresso.

It's the same deal with banks. Look for low fees, high accessibility (like lots of ATMs and good online banking), stellar customer service, and the best interest rates. And here's a pro tip: don't overlook credit unions. They're like the local cafés of banking—often more personalized than big banks, and they might offer better rates and lower fees because they're nonprofit.

When you set up your accounts, please consider how you like to access your money. Do you prefer chatting with tellers, or are you all about banking from your smartphone at midnight? Make sure your bank matches your lifestyle. Most banks now offer robust online banking services, which can be a game-changer. They let you pay bills online, transfer money between accounts, and even deposit checks through your phone. Plus, it's a great way to keep an eye on your money; you can check your balances and recent transactions anytime, anywhere—super handy for spotting anything fishy.

Speaking of fishy, let's talk security. Keeping your bank accounts safe in the digital age is more important than ever. Start with the basics like choosing strong, unique passwords for your online banking accounts—no, "password123" won't cut it. Consider using a password manager to keep track of them all. Be on the lookout for phishing attempts, usually emails or messages that trick you into giving away personal info by pretending to be your bank. Remember, a genuine bank will never ask for your password or PIN by email. Always use secure, private Wi-Fi when accessing your bank accounts online—no checking your balance at the local coffee shop's public Wi-Fi.

So there you have it, your crash course in basic banking. Whether you're depositing your first paycheck, saving for a new laptop, or just trying to keep a closer eye on where your money's going, these tips should help you navigate the waters of personal banking. Stick to these fundamentals, and you'll be on your way to becoming a savvy banker. Remember, every tremendous financial strategy starts with understanding the basics, so take these lessons and put them to good use.

1.4 SETTING UP YOUR FINANCIAL TOOLKIT: APPS AND PLATFORMS

In the digital age, managing your finances can be as easy as posting a selfie or swiping right. Thanks to many savvy apps and platforms, you can now budget, invest, save, and track your spending from your smartphone or laptop. If you spend hours on your phone, you can make some of that time financially productive. Here's a rundown of tools to turn financial chaos into a well-organized concert of numbers and goals.

First off, let's talk about budgeting apps. These nifty little helpers can automate much of the work of managing your daily expenses and income. Apps like Rocket Money and YNAB (You Need A Budget) track and categorize your spending to see exactly where that money is going—be it mouth-watering burgers or those sneaky little online subscriptions. They sync up with your bank accounts and credit cards, pulling in your latest transactions and categorizing them into neat charts and graphs. Imagine having a financial dashboard that shows you, in real-time, just how much of your monthly budget has been gobbled up by takeout or how close you are to hitting your savings goals. It's like having a financial advisor in your pocket, minus the hourly fees.

Now, onto the investment apps. If you've ever felt investing is a rich person's game, think again. Apps like Acorns and Robinhood democratize investing, making it accessible to anyone with a smartphone. With Acorns, you can start small—really small. The app rounds up your daily purchases to the nearest dollar and invests the difference. So, every time you buy a coffee for $3.75, Acorns tosses $0.25 into an investment account. It's painless and gradual, so you're building an investment portfolio without trying too hard. On the other hand, Robinhood lets you dive into the world of stocks, ETFs, and even cryptocurrencies without needing to pay commissions or own full shares. Want to own a piece of Apple or Tesla but don't have thousands to invest? No problem. Robinhood lets you buy fractional shares with as much money as you're willing to spend. Not interested in managing stocks? Warren Buffett (a famous investor) recommends just buying SPY, an exchange-traded fund (ETF) that invests in the 500 largest stocks on the S&P 500. This is easy to do, and the ETF has a low cost of managing the invested funds. It saves you the time and hassle of researching and buying stocks that can change drastically overnight.

But great power comes with great responsibility, especially when using these tools effectively. It's not just about having them; it's about making them work for you. For budgeting apps, take the time to set up detailed budgets that reflect your actual income and lifestyle. Be honest about your regular expenses and financial goals. The more accurate your input, the more valuable the insights you'll get. For investment apps, start by defining your risk tolerance and investment goals. Are you saving for a short-term goal, like a vacation next year, or are you looking at long-term growth for retirement? Each goal might require different strategies and different apps.

Embracing these tools can lead to better financial habits. Regularly checking your budgeting app, for instance, can help curb impulsive buys when you see your budget categories filling up. Watching your investments grow in real time can motivate you to invest and manage your money wisely. It's about being proactive, not reactive. When you start paying attention to where your money is going and how it's growing, you set the stage for a future where financial crises are things you read about, not experience firsthand.

So, there you have it: a digital financial toolkit at your fingertips, ready to help you take control of your money. Whether you're a seasoned saver or a finance newbie, these apps and platforms can offer insights and assistance that were once only available to professional investors or those with a fleet of advisors. Go ahead, download a few, and start tinkering around. With each swipe, tap, and click, you're not just passing the time—you're paving your way to a more secure financial future.

1.5 DECODING FINANCIAL JARGON: SIMPLIFYING COMPLEX TERMS

Have you ever found yourself nodding to a financial advisor's spiel, only to realize you didn't understand the meaning behind half the terms they used? You're not alone. Financial jargon can sound like a foreign language, but fear not! I'm here to break it down into snackable pieces so you can talk the talk and walk the walk. Let's demystify some of these terms with plain language and everyday analogies, transforming them from head-scratchers into clear concepts to make smarter financial decisions.

First, let's tackle APR, or the annual percentage rate. Imagine shopping for a new smartphone and seeing two payment options: pay $600 upfront or $50 monthly for a year under a financing plan. If you do the math, $50 times 12 months equals $600. So, is it the exact cost either way? Not so fast. The financing option often includes interest, represented as the APR, which means you pay more than $600. APR is that extra cost spread over the year, allowing you to evaluate if paying over time is worth the additional cost compared to paying upfront.

Next, let's decode **amortization**. Think of it like a pizza. You buy a large pizza (a loan) and decide to eat it (pay it off) slice by slice over the next year. Amortization is simply the plan of how you eat (pay) each slice (portion of the loan), usually in equal parts, so you know exactly how much pizza (debt) you have left at any time and when you'll be all done. Each payment includes a bit of the principal (the original amount of the loan) and interest, ensuring that by the end of the term, your pizza is completely eaten (and your loan is fully paid off).

Moving on to **equity**. Let's say you and a friend decide to buy a fancy espresso machine together because you can't live without your daily caffeine fix. You both pay half the price and own half the machine. Your share of the ownership of the espresso machine is your equity. In financial terms, equity is often used in home ownership, referring to how much of your house you own. If your home is worth $300,000 and you have a mortgage of $200,000, your equity in the house is $100,000.

Lastly, we have **liquidity**. Imagine you're a collector of rare comic books. While you might own $5,000 worth of comics, if you needed cash quickly, you couldn't necessarily sell them right away for their total value. Liquidity refers to how quickly you can turn assets into cash. Cold, hard cash is super liquid – it's already cash. But other things, like your comic books or even real estate, take more time to convert to money, making them less liquid.

Understanding these terms isn't just academic; it has real-world applications that can affect your daily financial decisions. For instance, knowing the APR on your credit card can help you understand how much extra you'll pay if you carry a balance.

Understanding amortization can affect how you approach your mortgage payments, potentially saving you thousands in interest over time. Recognizing your assets' liquidity is crucial when planning for emergencies and knowing how quickly you can access cash.

To keep all these terms straight, here's a handy glossary to refer back to whenever you come across a financial term that makes you go, "Huh?":

- **APR (Annual Percentage Rate):** The yearly cost of borrowing money, expressed as a percentage.
- **Amortization:** Paying off a debt over time through regular payments.
- **Equity:** The difference between the value of an asset (your home) and the amount of any liabilities (your mortgage) on that asset.
- **Liquidity:** The ease with which an asset can be converted into cash without affecting its market price.

By getting comfortable with this jargon, you're better equipped to navigate the financial world, avoid pitfalls, and take control of your economic destiny. After all, knowledge is power, especially regarding your money. So, next time you review a loan agreement or investment prospectus, you won't just nod and smile; you'll understand precisely what's on the table, making you a savvier investor and a more informed consumer. Whether it's negotiating the terms of a mortgage, understanding investment opportunities, or simply discussing your financial plans, mastering this jargon will serve you well throughout your financial adventures.

CHAPTER 2
MASTERING CASH FLOW AND DEBT MANAGEMENT

So, you've been riding the financial rollercoaster, and let's be honest, the thrill of unpredictability is wearing off. You're ready to get off this wild ride and onto something a bit more stable —like maybe a financial merry-go-round that lets you enjoy the scenery without the risk of losing your lunch. Welcome to mastering cash flow and managing debt, where getting a grip on your income and expenditures can turn that stomach-churning loop-de-loop into a pleasant spin.

2.1 STRATEGIES FOR LIVING BEYOND PAYCHECK TO PAYCHECK

Cutting Back Without Cutting Out Fun

Let's start with some financial detox—nothing too scary, just a simple audit of your spending habits. Think of it like cleaning out your fridge. You want to get rid of the moldy cheese and those questionable leftovers but keep the good stuff that nourishes you. Similarly, take a good, hard look at your expenses. What's eating up your cash? Maybe it's those impromptu gourmet coffee runs or the gym membership you barely use. It's time to trim the fat.

Start by tracking everything you spend for a month—even that $2 soda. You can use an app or kick old school with a notebook. Whatever works for you! As you categorize your expenses, you'll spot the easy cuts. Maybe choose a less expensive gym or swap out several dine-outs for cozy home-cooked meals. Remember, it's not about depriving yourself but about making smarter choices that keep your wallet and your soul fully fed.

Structuring Your Spending Like a Pro

Let's talk about structure because a little framework can bring peace. Divide your income into straightforward categories: needs, wants, savings, and debts. It's like organizing your closet. Needs are your staple items—rent, utilities, groceries. Wants are the fun but not essential extras—streaming subscriptions, fashion, gadgets. Here's a pro tip: aim to spend about 50% on needs and 30% on wants, and stash away 20% for savings and debt repayment. This formula isn't set in stone, but it's a great starting point to tailor.

Diversify Your Income Like Your Investment Portfolio

If living paycheck to paycheck is your main issue, let's jazz up your income streams. Think of your income like a band. If you only have one musician, it's cool, but it could be improved. Now, imagine having a drummer, a guitarist, and a keyboardist. Suddenly, you've got a richer, fuller sound.

In the same way, consider picking up a side hustle or diving into the gig economy. Freelance writing, graphic design, or even tutoring can become lucrative gigs that supplement your income. Make sure these gigs harmonize with your lifestyle and career goals.

Prioritizing Expenses: Needs Before Wants

Finally, prioritizing your expenditures helps balance the scales. It's about getting your financial priorities straight. Always cover your essentials first. Missing a rent payment is like skipping a beat—everything gets off rhythm. Once your necessities are paid, then you can allocate funds to less critical expenses and, of course, fun stuff. And yes, fun is necessary too—just after the electricity bill. This method keeps you solvent and eases stress, knowing everything essential is covered. Plus, it teaches you the invaluable skill of discernment, enhancing your financial decision-making in the long haul.

Reflection Section: Your Financial Priorities

Please take a moment to reflect on what you value most in your spending. What are some essentials that you cannot live without? Now, think about what you enjoy but could cut back on. This exercise isn't about cutting joy out of your life but rather about creating a balance that ensures your financial health and personal happiness. Write down three financial priorities that you believe are essential and three areas where you can cut back. This will help guide your budgeting decisions and ensure your spending aligns with your values and financial goals.

2.2 SMART DEBT HANDLING: CREDIT CARDS AND STUDENT LOANS

Navigating the maze of credit card offers and student loan statements can feel like trying to solve a Rubik's cube blindfolded. But don't worry, I've got the cheat codes that'll help you manage these debts without breaking a sweat. Let's start with credit cards. They're not just plastic rectangles in your wallet; they're powerful financial tools that can help or hinder your financial journey, depending on how you use them.

First, let's debunk a common myth: having a credit card does not mean free money! Think of it more like a loan shark in your pocket. It's convenient and can help in a pinch, but it can bite. You must be careful. The golden rule here is simple: always aim to pay off your balance in full each month. This avoids interest charges, which can stack up faster than dirty laundry in a dorm room. If you can't pay in full, pay more than the minimum to chip away at the principal faster, reducing the interest you pay over time. And speaking of interest, always be aware of your card's APR (annual percentage rate). Lower is better, but understanding the rate can help you prioritize which card to pay off first if you're juggling balances on multiple cards.

Next up, let's talk rewards. Credit card rewards can be a nice cherry on top if you pay your balance in full each month without incurring interest. Cashback, points, travel miles—these perks can save money or enhance your life if used wisely. However, choosing cards with rewards that match your lifestyle is crucial. There's no point in racking up travel miles if you're a homebody, right? Instead, maybe a card that offers cash back on groceries or gas would be more up your alley. Always read the fine print and understand the terms to maximize these benefits without falling into spending traps to earn points.

Now, let's shift gears to another beast: student loans. If you're like many young adults, student loans are a significant part of your financial landscape. Managing them doesn't have to be a nightmare, though. You'll be able to start by understanding your repayment options. The standard plan is only sometimes the best fit for everyone, especially if you're starting out and still need to make the big bucks. Income-driven repayment plans can be a lifesaver, adjusting your monthly payments based on your income and family size. This can make your payments more manageable and prevent you from choosing between paying your loan or eating more than instant noodles for dinner.

Another avenue worth exploring is loan forgiveness programs. Yes, they exist, and no, they're not a myth! Work in specific public service jobs. You might qualify for forgiveness of the remaining balance on your Direct Loans after you've made 120 qualifying payments under a qualifying repayment plan. It's like the government's saying, "Thanks for helping out; here's a little something to lighten your load." Research these options and see if you qualify—it could save you significant change.

Lastly, keeping track of your debt might sound like something other than the most thrilling activity, but it's essential. Use apps and tools that consolidate all your debt information in one place. Seeing everything at a glance—not just your student loans but also your credit cards and other debts—can give you a clear picture of where you stand and help you make informed payment decisions. Some apps even suggest the best strategies for repayment based on your specific debts and financial situation, taking a lot of the guesswork out of the equation.

By tackling your debts head-on with these strategies, you're not just avoiding collectors and maintaining your credit score—you're setting yourself up for a more accessible, flexible financial future. Whether leveraging credit card rewards to your advantage or navigating the complex world of student loans, remember that knowledge is your most powerful tool. Use it well, and watch as those daunting debts transform into manageable parts of your financial portfolio.

2.3 NEGOTIATING BETTER TERMS ON EXISTING DEBTS

Ever felt like your debts are like that clingy friend who won't take a hint to leave? Well, it's time to learn the art of negotiation, not just to manage your clingy friends but, more importantly, your even clingier debts. Negotiating with creditors might sound as daunting as asking for a raise. Still, with the right approach, you can successfully lower your interest rates or consolidate your debts into more manageable terms. Think of it as haggling at a flea market, but you could save hundreds or even thousands in interest payments instead of walking away with a vintage lamp.

First up, let's sharpen those negotiation skills. The key is preparation. Before you pick up the phone, gather all your debt information—know how much you owe, the interest rates, and your payment history. Good or bad, this info will guide your conversation. Now, it's game time. When you call your creditor, be polite but assertive. Start by explaining your situation honestly. Maybe you've hit a rough patch, or you're just looking for a way to manage your payments better. Then, make your move—ask if they can lower your interest rate or offer a more flexible repayment plan. Remember, creditors usually prefer to get paid less over a more extended period than not get paid at all. It's surprising how often they're willing to work with you, especially if you've been a good customer.

But what if the usual chit-chat doesn't cut it? That's where debt consolidation comes into play. This is like turning your closet full of assorted debts into a neatly organized wardrobe with just one or two main pieces. You take out a new loan with a lower interest rate to pay off your other debts. This can simplify your life with a single payment each month and potentially lower your interest charges. However, tread carefully—ensure the terms genuinely benefit you before diving in. Sometimes, the costs hidden in the folds of these deals can outweigh the benefits. After you have consolidated, you must promise not to open another credit card. Just use your debit card to only spend what you have in the bank.

Suppose you're considering refinancing, especially for hefty burdens like student loans or high-interest credit card debts; timing and options matter. Refinancing your student loans might lower your payments and interest rate, but beware of losing benefits like loan forgiveness or flexible repayment options available with federal loans. As for credit cards, transferring your balance to a new card with a 0% introductory rate can give you a window to pay down your balance without accruing more interest. Just watch out for transfer fees and make sure you can clear the debt before the higher rate kicks in.

Navigating these conversations and decisions isn't just about crunching numbers; it's about communicating effectively. If you're struggling, don't wait until you've missed payments. Reach out to your creditors and explain your situation. Use clear, concise language and be upfront about what you can realistically afford. Sometimes, showing that you're proactive can make creditors more willing to negotiate. And if you're feeling overwhelmed, don't hesitate to bring a debt counselor into the mix. These pros can offer invaluable advice and might even handle negotiations for you. They know the ins and outs of debt management and can often wrangle concessions that might not have crossed your mind.

While negotiating your debt might seem like teaching a cat to sit, you can significantly improve your financial situation with the proper preparation and approach. It's about taking control, one conversation at a time, and turning those daunting debts into manageable commitments. Whether you're smoothing out your interest rates, consolidating your debts, or simply trying to get a better handle on your payments, remember that the goal is to create a system that works for you—one that lets you sleep a little easier at night, knowing your financial future is becoming more secure with every intelligent decision you make.

2.4 INNOVATIVE WAYS TO INCREASE YOUR INCOME

In this ever-evolving economy, sticking to just one income source can feel like putting all your eggs in one slightly unreliable basket. Let's shake things up and explore modern, creative ways to boost your cash flow. The gig economy, for instance, isn't just a buzzword

—it's a buffet of opportunities where you can pick up side gigs that fill your wallet and fit seamlessly into your lifestyle. Think about it: platforms like Upwork or Freelancer open doors to jobs from around the globe that you can tackle from your living room. Whether you're crafting killer blog posts, designing sleek logos, or helping someone halfway across the world learn English, these gigs can pad your bank account while you're still in your pajamas.

Let's talk about spinning your skills and passions into gold through entrepreneurship. Starting a business sounds daunting, but it doesn't have to be the next Google to be successful. It's about spotting and filling a need, even on a small scale. Take Sara, for example, who started a mobile pet grooming service. With just a van, some pet grooming tools, and her love for dogs, she turned a side hustle into a thriving business that brings in double what she made at her day job. The key? Start small. Think about what you can do with minimal upfront investment. Whether selling handmade jewelry on Etsy, launching a drop-shipping store, or starting a blog, low-cost startups are an excellent way to dip your toes into entrepreneurial waters.

As you hustle and bustle, don't forget about the gold mine that is professional development. Investing in your skills can lead to promotions or even new job opportunities with a heftier paycheck. And no, it doesn't always mean returning to school for another degree. Online platforms like Coursera and Udemy offer courses on everything from coding to project management—skills that could significantly increase your market value. Just imagine that a few hours a week could transform your career trajectory, leading to roles you've only dreamed of. It's like leveling up in a video game, except the points you score are dollars.

Lastly, let's unpack the idea of passive income because the money that makes itself is as sweet as it sounds. Passive income comes in many flavors, but let's focus on two: dividend stocks and rental properties. Dividend stocks are like gifts that keep on giving. Invest in a solid stock, and you can receive regular dividends just for holding onto it. It's a way to benefit from a company's profits without getting involved in the day-to-day grind. Then there's real estate. Purchasing a rental property can provide a steady income stream that pays for itself and contributes to your savings. Sure, being a landlord comes with its challenges, but with platforms like Airbnb, you can rent out even a portion of your home for short periods for some quick cash.

Embracing these income-generating strategies can transform your financial landscape from barren to brimming. It's about making money work for you, diversifying your income streams, and taking proactive steps toward financial independence. So why settle for a financial trickle when you can turn on the tap and let the opportunities flow? Whether through freelancing, entrepreneurship, upskilling, or intelligent investments, the doors are wide open. It's up to you to step through them and claim your slice of the financial pie.

2.5 MANAGING RECURRING PAYMENTS AND SUBSCRIPTIONS

Let's face it: in the age of subscriptions and automated payments, our finances can sometimes feel like they're on autopilot and not always in a good way. You sign up for a free trial, forget to cancel, and suddenly, you're a premium member of the 'Jelly of the Month Club.' It's not precisely the investment of the century. Managing these recurring payments doesn't just save you money—it brings back a sense of control. Let's dive into some strategies to keep these sneaky expenses in check and ensure you only spend on what truly adds value to your life.

Keeping Subscriptions in Check

First, auditing your ongoing subscriptions is like doing a spring clean; it's about keeping what brings you joy and ditching the rest. Start by listing all your subscriptions—streaming services, gym memberships, and app subscriptions that seemed like a good idea then. Now, evaluate each one. How often do you use it? Is it worth the cost? This isn't just about cutting costs but about optimizing your spending. You might find that some subscriptions are worth every penny because of the value or enjoyment they bring to your life. Others, however, might silently drain your bank account without offering much in return. Apps like Rocket Money or Hiatus can help by tracking your subscriptions and highlighting those you might have forgotten. They can even assist in the cancellation process, making cutting the cords less hassle.

Automating the Smart Way

While some automation can lead to unnecessary spending, setting up automatic payments for the subscriptions or bills you decide to keep can be a financial lifesaver. Think of it as putting your financial responsibilities on a reliable schedule. This saves time and helps avoid late fees, which can sneak up and bite you in the budget. Automating your essential payments ensures that your must-haves are taken care of, allowing you to focus on other financial goals without worrying about missing a payment. Plus, many service providers offer small discounts for setting up auto-pay so that they can save a few dollars along the way, too.

Negotiating Like a Pro

Talking about saving dollars, let's not forget the power of negotiation. Yes, you can negotiate the cost of recurring services like internet, phone plans, and even some subscriptions. Start by researching what competitors are offering. Call your provider and tell them if you find a better deal elsewhere. Be polite but firm. Explain that you're considering switching unless they match or beat the competitor's price. You'd be surprised how often they are willing to offer a discount to keep you as a customer. And if you're uncomfortable negotiating independently, services like Billshark or Trim can do the legwork for you. They often take a percentage of the savings they earn you, but if they don't save you money, you don't pay.

2.6 EMERGENCY FUNDS: HOW MUCH AND HOW SOON

Think of an emergency fund as your financial safety net, designed to catch you when a sudden job loss, a medical crisis, or a car breakdown threatens to throw you off your financial high wire. It's not about if these situations will happen—it's about being prepared when they do. Having an emergency fund is like keeping a spare tire in your trunk; hopefully, you won't need it, but boy, aren't you relieved when it's there?

Now, how much should you stash away in this safety net? A good rule is to aim for three to six months' living expenses. But before you panic at the figure, remember, this isn't about pulling a rabbit out of a hat. It's about building up to it gradually. Calculate what you typically spend monthly on absolute necessities—rent, food, utilities, and transport—got that number? That's your one-month target. Multiply that by three, or hey, go for six if you want extra peace of mind, and you've got your ultimate savings goal.

So, where do you keep this fund? Under the mattress or in a shoebox might sound temptingly old-school, but let's get you into the 21st century with something that earns you interest while keeping your cash accessible. High-yield savings accounts are perfect for this. They offer better interest rates than standard accounts, meaning your emergency fund grows while you sleep without locking up your money when needed. These accounts balance earning potential and accessibility, precisely what you want for an emergency fund.

Ready to start funneling money into your emergency fund? Here's how you can begin today, even if your budget is tighter than a new pair of shoes. First, automate your savings. Set up a direct transfer from your checking account to your emergency fund right after payday—think of it as paying your future self first. Even a tiny amount, like $50 or $100 a month, adds up. Next, whenever you get extra cash—a bonus, tax refund, or even birthday money—resist the urge to splurge and allocate a portion of it to your emergency fund. It's about taking small, manageable steps that lead to significant strides in your financial security.

Building an emergency fund doesn't need to be a Herculean task. By breaking it down into achievable goals, choosing the right place to store it, and committing to regular contributions, you're paving your way to financial resilience. Remember, this fund is more than just money—it's peace of mind, a buffer against life's uncertainties, allowing you to face financial challenges without derailing your long-term goals.

As this chapter wraps up, we've armed you with strategies to manage your cash flow effectively, tackle debt head-on, and boost your income through innovative avenues. More importantly, we've emphasized the indispensable role of an emergency fund in fortifying your financial foundation. Each step, from cutting unnecessary expenses to diversifying your income streams, is geared towards building a robust financial buffer that shields you from life's unexpected downturns.

Moving forward, the journey into the intricacies of investing and growing your wealth awaits. We'll demystify the world of stocks, bonds, and real estate and guide you through creating investments that preserve and enhance your financial well-being. Stay tuned because mastering your finances is just starting, and the best is yet to come.

CHAPTER 3
INVESTING AND GROWING YOUR WEALTH

Alright, strap in! We're about to take a wild ride into the world of investing. Now, before you picture many old guys in suits shouting over each other on the stock market floor, let me stop you. This is investing for you and me—the everyday adventurers looking to grow their stash of cash with some smart moves and a sprinkle of daring. Think of this as your gateway to turning those hard-earned dollars into a mountain of money (okay, maybe more like a pleasant hill to begin with).

3.1 STOCKS AND BONDS: INVESTING 101 FOR BEGINNERS

What in the World are Stocks and Bonds?

Let's start with the basics. Imagine you're at a giant marketplace, but instead of buying fruit and veggies, you're buying tiny pieces of companies. These pieces are called stocks. When you own a stock, you own a part of that company. If the company does well, the value of your stock goes up. If it doesn't, you might not be as happy about that. It's like fantasy football, but you're betting on companies instead of betting on players.

Now, bonds are a bit different. Think of them as a loan you give to a company or government; they promise to pay you back with interest after a certain period. It's like lending money to your friend who needs to buy a fancy new bike and then getting back more money than you lent. Stocks are about owning a piece, and bonds are about being owed money.

Making Your First Moves in the Market

So, how do you get started? First, you'll need a brokerage account and your ticket to the investment party. Setting one up is as easy as signing up for a streaming service, except you get access to the stock market instead of movies. Once your account is ready, it's time to buy some stocks or bonds. You can choose individual stocks if you've got a good feeling about a particular company or go for bonds if you like the idea of a safer bet.

You'll encounter terms like 'market orders' and 'limit orders' when placing an order. A market order is like saying, "I'll take that stock at whatever price it is when the market executes my order." A limit where you specify the price, saying, "I want this stock, but only if I can pay $50 or less." It's a way to ensure you don't overpay when stock prices bounce around like a kangaroo on a trampoline.

Why You Shouldn't Put All Your Eggs in One Basket

Now, let's talk about diversification. It's a fancy term for not putting all your eggs in one basket. Instead of betting everything on one stock or bond, you spread your investments across different types. Why? Because investing is unpredictable. One lousy event shouldn't have the power to wipe out your entire investment. By spreading your money out, you reduce the risk of one bad apple spoiling the whole bunch.

Real-Life Wins: The Simplicity of ETFs

Let's look at a real-world example—ETFs or Exchange-Traded Funds. Think of an ETF as a basket of stocks or bonds. Instead of picking and choosing individual stocks, you buy a share of the ETF, which includes a little piece of everything in the basket. It's like buying a pre-made smoothie instead of blending each fruit yourself. One popular ETF is the SPY, which includes a slice of the top 500 companies in the U.S. It's a simple way to dive into investing without analyzing every stock out there.

By starting with these basics, you're setting yourself up not just to play the game but to play it well. Stocks and bonds might sound like grown-up stuff, and they are, but they're also your tools for building a future where money is a resource, not a roadblock. Whether you're rolling in dough or just starting to build your financial empire, understanding and participating in investing can be your ticket to a more secure and exciting financial life. So, why wait? Dive into the deep end, and let's make your money work for you!

3.2 RETIREMENT ACCOUNTS: STARTING IN YOUR 20S

Imagine you're planting a tree. The best time to grow it was 20 years ago, but the next best time? Today. That's how you should think about saving for retirement. It may seem like a distant future event, but starting in your 20s can be a game-changer, thanks to a bit of magic called compound interest. This isn't just regular interest; it's interest on your interest. It's like your money is having babies, and those babies are having babies, and so on—creating a family tree of dollars. The sooner you start, the more time your money has to grow and the less you have to save each month to reach your retirement goals. It's the difference between sprinting and taking a stroll to the same destination; starting earlier means enjoying the journey without getting winded.

Now, let's talk about where to stash this growing family of funds. You've got a few options for retirement accounts, each with its perks and quirks. The 401(k) is one of the most well-known, often offered through employers. If your job provides one, jumping on that bandwagon is a no-brainer, especially if there's a company match. Think of a company match as free money. It's like your boss saying, "Hey, I liked that you saved some of your paycheck, so here's a bit more to help you out!" Not all superheroes wear capes; some contribute to your 401(k).

But what if you're flying solo or your workplace doesn't offer a retirement plan? That's where Individual Retirement Accounts (IRAs) come into play. Traditional IRAs let you make pre-tax contributions, reducing your taxable income now and letting your investments grow tax-deferred until you retire. Then there's the Roth IRA, the cool younger sibling, which flips the script. You pay taxes on your contributions upfront, but when it's time to retire, every penny you pull out is yours, tax-free. It's perfect if you expect to be in a higher tax bracket later on or want the peace of mind of knowing that your retirement withdrawals won't be taxed.

How much should you be socking away in these accounts? While a general rule of thumb is to aim for 15% of your income, start with what you can manage, even if it's just 1%. The key is consistency and gradually increasing your contributions as your salary grows. If your employer offers a 401(k) match, try to contribute enough at least to get the full match; it's an immediate 100% return on your investment.

Let's visualize the impact of these early investments. Imagine two friends, Alex and Taylor. Alex starts putting $200 a month into her retirement account at age 25, while Taylor does the same at age 35. Even if they both earn the same average annual return of 7%, by the time they hit retirement at age 65, Alex will have $528,225 in her account, while Taylor will only have $245,618, all because she gave her money more time to grow through compound interest. It clearly illustrates why starting early can make such a huge difference; it's not just about how much you save but how long it has to grow.

By embracing these retirement savings strategies now, you're setting yourself up for a future where work is optional and financial stress is minimal. Whether navigating the world of 401(k)s, diving into the specifics of IRAs, or figuring out how much of your paycheck to allocate to your monthly retirement, the key is to start as soon as possible. Your future self will thank you for the early start, and your retirement could look more like a well-deserved extended vacation than a financial scramble. So plant that tree today, and watch your retirement savings flourish.

3.3 REAL ESTATE AS AN INVESTMENT: WHAT YOU NEED TO KNOW

So, you're thinking about diving into the world of real estate investment, huh? Buckle up because it's a bit like playing Monopoly in real life but with more paperwork and less chance of going to jail for landing on someone's hotel. Real estate can be a fantastic way to build wealth, whether buying up residential spaces to rent out or eyeing that sleek commercial property downtown. But as with any game, knowing the rules and strategies can make the difference between booming success and a bank-account-busting blunder.

Getting Down with the Basics

First things first, we should lay down some groundwork. Real estate investment can broadly be split into two main categories: residential and commercial. Residential properties are all about those spaces where people live—think apartments, houses, and duplexes. On the other hand, commercial real estate includes office spaces, retail locations, and warehouses—places where people do business. Each type has its perks and quirks, so choosing the right kind can depend on your investment goals, budget, and how much you enjoy dealing with midnight calls about busted water pipes (a common joy of residential rentals).

Now, onto some key terms that every budding real estate mogul should know:

- **Cash Flow**: This is the lifeblood of your real estate investment. It's the net amount of cash the property generates, typically monthly, after all expenses are paid. Positive cash flow means you're making more money than spending on mortgage payments, maintenance, and other costs, precisely where you want to be.
- **Capital Appreciation**: This is the increase in the value of your property over time due to changes in the market and improvements you make to the property. It's like buying a fixer-upper, turning it into a gem, and selling it at a price that makes your wallet much heavier.
- **Leverage**: In real estate terms, leverage is using borrowed capital (like a mortgage) to increase the potential return of an investment. It means you're using other people's money to make more for yourself. High-risk, high-reward kind of deal.

Evaluating Your Potential Goldmine

Choosing the right property is like picking your team in dodgeball —you want the best players to win. When evaluating real estate investments, location tops the list. A prime spot can mean the difference between a property always in demand and one that sits empty, collecting dust. Look for areas with growing job markets, good schools, and amenities like parks and shopping centers. Market trends also play a huge role. Is the area up-and-coming, or is it on the decline? Keeping an eye on these trends can help you buy low and sell high, maximizing your capital appreciation.

Another critical factor is rental yield, the annual rental income expressed as a percentage of the property's total cost. High yield means the property can pay for itself over time through the rent you collect, making it a juicy target for your investment dollars. Also, consider the total return on investment, which combines rental yield and capital appreciation to give you the complete picture of what your money is doing for you.

Financing the Dream

Unless you're swimming in cash, you'll likely need some financing to get your real estate empire off the ground. Traditional mortgages are the most common route, offering relatively low interest rates and extended repayment terms. But an FHA loan might be your ticket if you're looking at a property that needs some love (a.k.a. a fixer-upper). These loans are backed by the government and are designed to help homeowners who want to renovate their digs.

For those who want to invest in real estate but prefer not to get their hands dirty, real estate investment trusts (REITs) or crowdfunding platforms like Fundrise offer a way to do so without managing properties directly. These options pool money from multiple investors to buy properties and then pay out dividends from the rental income and profits from property sales.

The Balancing Act: Risks and Rewards

Like any investment, real estate comes with risks and rewards. On the plus side, properties can provide steady cash flow and appreciate over time, offering an excellent return when you sell. Real estate can also be a hedge against inflation, as property values and rents typically increase with it.

However, it's not all sunshine and rent checks. Managing properties can be time-consuming and stressful—tenants can be difficult, repairs can be costly, and vacancies can drain your finances. Market downturns can also reduce property values and rental demand, leaving you with less income or property worth less than you paid.

But don't let the risks scare you off. Real estate can be a hugely rewarding investment with careful planning, a clear understanding of the market, and a bit of savvy. Whether buying your first rental property or looking to expand your portfolio, the key is to do your homework, plan for the unexpected, and always keep an eye on the long-term horizon.

3.4 ETHICAL AND IMPACT INVESTING FOR A BETTER WORLD

So, you want to make money and feel good about it simultaneously? Welcome to the world of ethical and impact investing, where your dollars fight the good fight, backing companies and funds that prioritize social responsibility, environmental stewardship, and corporate governance. Think of it as investing with a conscience, ensuring your investments align with your values without sacrificing returns. It's like having your cake and eating it, too, but the cake also helps plant trees and supports fair labor practices.

Ethical investing often avoids companies that harm the environment, exploit labor, or engage in unethical practices. Instead, it channels funds into businesses that contribute positively to the world. This could mean investing in a company that's pioneering clean energy solutions or renowned for its stellar human rights record. Impact investing takes it a step further by actively seeking to make a positive impact—think of it as investing to get a great return and solve social or environmental problems. It's an investment strategy that recognizes the power of money to change the world for the better.

Exploring the Landscape of Ethical and Impact Investments

Now, let's talk about how you can get involved. The array of options is broader than you might think. Environmental, Social, and Governance (ESG) funds are popular. These funds assess companies based on specific criteria: environmental impact (how green the company is), social responsibility (how it treats people), and governance (how the company is run). Investing in ESG funds means putting your money into companies that score high on these aspects, which can be a great way to ensure your investments reflect your ethics.

Green bonds are another exciting option. These bonds specifically fund projects with environmental benefits, like renewable energy developments or clean transportation initiatives. They're like giving a high-five to the planet with your investment dollars. Then, there are socially responsible mutual funds, which pool money from various investors to buy stocks in socially responsible companies. These funds not only aim for financial returns but also ensure that investments positively impact society.

Making Money While Making a Difference

You might wonder if focusing on ethics means compromising on returns. Good news: it doesn't have to. Studies have shown that companies concentrating on strong environmental, social, and governance practices can outperform their less scrupulous counterparts. They tend to attract better talent, have more loyal customers, and are even at a lower risk of regulatory fines—all of which can lead to better financial performance. It's a win-win: you support good causes and potentially improve your financial returns.

Success Stories from the Front Lines

Let's look at some real-world heroes of ethical investing. Consider the story of an investor who put money into a green bond issued by a city to upgrade its infrastructure to more sustainable technologies. The bond funded the installation of solar panels and energy-efficient buildings. Not only did the investor enjoy a steady interest income from the bond, but they also contributed to reducing the city's carbon footprint.

Another inspiring case is that of a mutual fund that invests in companies with progressive employment practices. One of the fund's picks was a tech company known for its excellent worker compensation and advancement practices. The company's strong performance and low employee turnover translated into impressive gains for the fund, proving that good ethics can lead to good returns.

Ethical and impact investing is more than a trend—it's a powerful movement towards more conscious capitalism, where financial gain meets global gain. By investing ethically, you're not just building wealth but helping create a better world. Whether you're drawn to the environmental focus of green bonds, the broad reach of ESG funds, or the targeted impact of socially responsible mutual funds, your investment choices can reflect your values and drive positive change. As you explore these opportunities, think of each investment as a vote for the kind of world you want to live in. Your portfolio can be a portfolio of change, impacting your finances and the planet's future. What could be more rewarding than that?

3.5 COMMON INVESTING MISTAKES AND HOW TO AVOID THEM

Let's face it: dipping your toes into the investment pool can sometimes feel like stepping into a game of financial Jenga. One wrong move and your stack of chips might wobble dangerously. It's cool, though, because I'm here to walk you through some common rookie investment mistakes and how to sidestep them like a pro dodging raindrops. So, grab your financial umbrella, and let's keep you dry from the investment downpour.

First up on the list of "oopsies" is investing without a plan. Picture this: you walk into a grocery store hungry, without a list. Chances are, you're going to throw a bunch of random stuff into your cart and end up with a hefty bill for food that doesn't even make one decent meal. Investing without a plan is similar. You might buy some stocks here and there because you heard a tip or they're trending on social media. Still, without a clear strategy or understanding of how these fit into your financial goals, you're potentially setting yourself up for a messy portfolio and disappointing results. The fix? Start with a goal. Whether saving for retirement, a down payment on a house, or building wealth, define what you want to achieve. Then, craft a plan that includes how much you need to invest, the types of assets that best suit your goals, and a timeline for your investments.

Next, let's talk about knee-jerk reactions to market fluctuations. The market is like a giant roller coaster—ups, downs, and some loop-de-loops. It's easy to panic when you see the market dip and think, "I've got to get out now!" But remember, investing is a marathon, not a sprint. Reacting impulsively to short-term market movement is like jumping off the roller coaster mid-ride—not a great idea. Instead, buckle up for the long haul. Keep a level head when the market gets rocky. Despite short-term volatility, the market has historically trended upward over the long term. If your investments are well-chosen and align with your long-term goals, staying the course is often the more intelligent route to take.

Speaking of being unprepared, entering the investment world without understanding your risk tolerance is like walking into a tattoo parlor and picking a random design off the wall. What seems like a fun idea now could lead to many regrets. Risk tolerance is about how much volatility you can handle without losing sleep. It varies from person to person and can change with your life circumstances. Assessing your risk tolerance involves understanding your financial situation, investment timeline, and emotional reaction to risk. Are you okay watching your portfolio dip 10% if there's a potential for higher returns, or would you prefer a more stable investment that grows slowly but surely? Understanding this will guide your investment choices and help you build a portfolio that fits your goals and your comfort level with risk.

Finally, there's the pitfall of not doing your homework. Investing in something you don't understand because it sounds cool or someone told you it's a hot tip is like eating a mystery dish at a buffet—you don't know what you're getting into, and it might not sit well. Constantly, and I mean continuously, research before you invest. Know what the company does, its financial health, market position, and growth potential. Use reputable sources to get your information, and if something sounds too good to be true, thoroughly investigate it.

By steering clear of these common mishaps, you're avoiding potential financial headaches and setting the stage for a healthier, wealthier portfolio that aligns beautifully with your life's goals and dreams. Remember, every investor makes mistakes, but the smart ones learn from them and use that knowledge to make better choices in the future. So, keep learning, planning, and adjusting your strategy as you go, and watch as your investment confidence and portfolio grow.

3.6 USING TECH TOOLS FOR SMARTER INVESTING

Imagine you've just been handed the keys to a supercar. It's sleek, powerful, and just waiting to tear up the track. But here's the catch: You've only driven something as fast as a golf cart. That's what jumping into investing feels like without the right tools. You have the power to accelerate your financial growth, but without the right tech tools and platforms, it's like trying to navigate the Autobahn with a blindfold. Let's take that blindfold off and look at how modern technology can turbo-charge your investing game.

Today's Investment platforms are like having a financial advisor, a data scientist, and a personal assistant rolled into one neat package right on your smartphone or laptop. These platforms offer a range of analytics tools, automated investing options, and personalized portfolio management features that can make your investing as hands-on or hands-off as you like. For instance, think about robo-advisors—these nifty tools use algorithms to manage your investments based on your risk tolerance and goals. They automatically adjust your portfolio to maximize gains or minimize losses depending on market conditions. It's like having a co-pilot constantly recalculating the best route to your financial destination.

Now, let's dive into some specifics. Take an app like Betterment or Wealthfront, which are frontrunners in the robo-advisor space. These apps invest your money based on sophisticated algorithms and rebalance your portfolio to keep it aligned with your goals. They consider age, investment goals, and risk tolerance to tailor your investments. The usability here is a big win—clean interfaces, straightforward navigation, and visual dashboards that show your investment growth over time. It's like watching your fitness progress on a workout app, but you're growing your cash instead of counting calories.

Using these tools effectively means engaging with them regularly. Set aside some time each week to check in on your investments. Look at the analytics to understand what's performing well and why. If you're using a robo-advisor, review its suggestions and adjust your settings if your financial situation or goals change. It is a regular tune-up to ensure your investment engine runs smoothly.

While these tools can make investing simpler and potentially more profitable, they also need heightened cybersecurity. Remember, you're dealing with sensitive personal and financial information. Ensuring the security of this data is crucial. Opt for investment platforms that offer two-factor authentication, use strong, unique passwords for each financial account, and consider using a dedicated device for your financial transactions. Keep an eye on your chosen platforms' security protocols and stay informed about the best practices for protecting your financial data online. It's a bit like locking your car in a bad neighborhood—it doesn't guarantee safety but significantly reduces risk.

By integrating these tech tools into your investment strategy, you're not just putting money into the market but placing a well-informed bet on your financial future. With the right tools, you can minimize guesswork, maximize efficiency, and keep a pulse on your financial health with a few clicks or taps. So, gear up, get your tools in order, and confidently drive your investments forward.

The road to financial independence is rarely a straight line. It twists and turns, and occasionally, there are potholes. But with the right strategies and tools, you can navigate it more smoothly. In this chapter, we've equipped you with the know-how to utilize cutting-edge technology to enhance your investing, ensuring you're not just on the road but accelerating down it. As we shift gears into the next chapter, we'll explore more ways to refine your investment strategies, ensuring every mile driven is one step closer to your ultimate destination: financial freedom. Hang tight; the journey continues!

CHAPTER 4

NAVIGATING LIFE CHANGES AND FINANCIAL DECISIONS

Remember when your most significant financial decision was choosing between an extra slice of pizza or saving that dollar for a rainy day arcade trip? Welcome to the big leagues, where the stakes are higher and your wallet feels lighter. College life: it's not just about acing exams and making lifelong friends; it's also a crash course in Managing Finances 101. Whether you're navigating the stormy seas of student loans or figuring out how to stretch those last few bucks over the weekend, I've got your back. Let's turn you into a budgeting ninja and a savvy saver, even if your current bank account balance makes you think twice about that extra coffee.

4.1 FINANCIAL PLANNING FOR COLLEGE STUDENTS

Budget Like a Boss

First up, let's talk budgeting. But not the kind that requires an advanced degree in spreadsheets or the patience of a saint. We're talking simple, straightforward budgeting that even the most finance-averse can handle. Could you start by tracking where your money goes each month? Yes, every single dollar. That includes the cash you spend on late-night snack runs and the ever-so-tempting campus coffee shop visits.

Here's the game plan: categorize your expenses. Essentials like rent, textbooks (more on saving here in a second), and food must be at the top of the list. Then, look at what's left for your 'wants'—like nights out with friends or the occasional concert. The trick isn't to cut out all the fun but to know where your money's going so you can make intelligent choices. Maybe swap a few dine-outs for potluck dinners with friends. Not only will your wallet thank you, but it's also a great way to test if you've learned anything in that cooking class.

Mastering Financial Aid: Loans, Grants, and Scholarships

Now, let's unravel the tangled web of financial aid. Loans, grants, scholarships—knowing how to manage these effectively can be the difference between a smooth college ride and a post-graduation debt hangover. First, exhaust all your 'free money' options—scholarships and grants you don't have to pay back. If you treat finding these like a part-time job, the payoff can mean thousands of dollars saved.

For the loans, here's the scoop: understand your terms. What's the interest rate? When do you need to start paying it back? Knowledge is power; the more you know about your loans, the better you can manage them. And if you do end up with a surplus in your financial aid, resist the urge to spend it on non-essentials. Think of it as an early investment in your debt-payoff plan.

Cost-Cutting Hacks: Save on Textbooks and More

Textbooks cost a small fortune, right? Here's a hack: don't buy new if you can avoid it. Rent, borrow, or buy used. Many campuses have textbook exchanges, or you can check out online sites that offer books for less. Consider living off-campus or getting a roommate to split the costs for housing. Every little bit that doesn't go into rent is something you can use elsewhere—or save.

Credit 101: Building Your Score Early

Lastly, let's touch on credit. Think of your credit score as your GPA for finances—it matters when you step into the 'real world.' Start with a student credit card, but use it wisely. Treat it like cash; if you can't pay off something by the end of the month, think twice before buying. Pay on time, keep your balances low and watch your credit score climb. It's like the financial version of leveling up.

Your Financial Toolkit: Apps and Platforms

Consider using a budgeting app tailored to students to keep all these financial balls in the air. Tools like Rocket Money or PocketGuard can help you track your spending, set budgets, and even remind you when to pay bills. Plus, seeing your cash flow in real-time can make managing your money less of a chore and more like a game—can you beat your high score from last month?

Navigating your college years financially doesn't have to feel like a trek through the wilderness. With the right tools, knowledge, and a proactive approach, you can manage your money like a pro, setting the stage for financial success long after turning your tassel. So, dive into these strategies, tweak them to fit your lifestyle, and watch your financial savvy grow alongside your academic achievements. Who says you can't have fun and be financially responsible? Not me. Let's prove them wrong, one wise financial decision at a time.

4.2 HANDLING FINANCES AFTER GRADUATION: WHAT'S NEXT?

So, you've tossed your cap, snagged that diploma, and now you're ready to conquer the world—or at least start paying off your student loans. Welcome to the world of adulting, where your financial decisions suddenly feel a lot more real. Let's talk about transitioning from the campus bubble to the full-blown real world, where your financial plans need a serious glow-up to match your new graduate status.

First up, student loans. If you're like most grads, you've got a mix of excitement about the future and a slight sense of dread looking at those loan statements. But here's the kicker—managing them smartly from the get-go can save you a bundle and a bunch of stress down the line. Start by understanding your grace period; that's the time you have before you need to start making payments. Use this period to get a grip on your finances rather than treating it as a holiday from reality. Consider different repayment plans—you might qualify for income-driven repayment or consolidation that can lower your monthly payments. And hey, if you land a job with a sweet paycheck, think about paying more than the minimum each month. It's like hitting fast-forward on a boring movie; you'll finish it sooner.

Now, let's talk about your first 'real' job and that thrilling moment when you get your first job offer. Salary negotiation isn't just for sales sharks or corporate moguls; it's for you, too. Don't just accept the first number thrown at you. Do your homework—know the average salary for your position in your industry and region. Sites like Glassdoor can be your best friends here. When you negotiate, think beyond just the dollar amount. Consider benefits like health insurance, retirement contributions, and even telecommuting options or flex hours. These can be just as valuable as a bump in your salary.

Setting financial goals post-graduation isn't just about paying bills and surviving; it's about thriving. Start setting up an emergency fund—aim for three to six months of living expenses. It's not flashy, but it's your financial safety net. Next, tackle high-interest debts like credit cards or private student loans. From there, consider saving for a down payment on a house or starting an investment portfolio. Remember, these goals don't have to be set in stone; they can evolve as your life does. It is essential to have a plan, stick to it, and adjust as you go.

Lastly, never stop learning—especially about finances. Graduating doesn't mean you know everything you need to manage your money effectively. The financial world is constantly changing, and staying on top of trends, new tools, and investment strategies can keep you one step ahead. Podcasts, books, blogs, and even following financial experts on social media can provide ongoing education that keeps your financial knowledge fresh.

Navigating life after graduation is more than finding a job and a place to live. It's about setting the stage for financial stability and success that lasts long into the future. You're doing more than just surviving the real world by managing your student loans wisely, mastering the art of salary negotiation, setting and adjusting your financial goals, and committing to lifelong financial learning. You're setting yourself up to thrive, ensuring that your post-college life is as rewarding financially as it is personally. So here's to turning those big dreams into reality, one wise financial decision at a time.

4.3 FINANCIAL CONSIDERATIONS FOR NEW COUPLES

So, you've found "the one," and you're ready to dive headfirst into the blissful waters of coupledom. But wait, there's more to it than just sunset walks and Netflix binges. Let's talk money because as much as love is the foundation of a great relationship, financial harmony can be the glue that keeps it all together. Navigating the financial conversation with your partner can be more relaxed than a wrong first date. It's all about transparency, setting the stage for a future where money talks are as regular as discussing your weekend plans.

First, let's break the ice on discussing finances openly. It's like pulling off a Band-Aid; sometimes, you must get it over with. Start with the basics: how much you earn, any debts (including those pesky student loans), and your financial goals. This isn't about judgment; it's about knowing where you both stand so you can plan your future together without any nasty surprises. Think of it as building a budget for two. You might find it helpful to schedule regular "money dates" to check in on your finances together, making it a part of your routine like your Sunday morning coffee run.

Now, onto the big question: to merge or not to merge finances? This is like deciding whether to move in together—it's a big step that can work out great, provided you're both on the same page. Merging finances can simplify things like paying bills and saving for shared goals (hello, dream vacation!), but it can also lead to friction if you have very different spending habits. On the flip side, keeping things separate gives you autonomy over your money, but it can make coordinating joint expenses more like a logistical puzzle. Some couples find a hybrid approach works best—joint accounts for shared expenses but separate accounts for personal spending. Whatever you decide, communication is critical. Make sure you both feel comfortable and secure with whatever financial arrangement you choose.

Planning for major purchases and investments is another hot topic. Whether buying a car, a house or investing in stocks, these are not decisions to make on a whim. Please sit down and discuss what each purchase means for your financial landscape. For instance, if buying a home is on the horizon, consider how much mortgage you can afford without putting undue stress on your other financial obligations. A good rule of thumb? Keep your mortgage below 28% of your combined take-home pay. This keeps your housing costs manageable while leaving room in your budget for other expenses (and fun stuff). When planning these enormous purchases, consider the future value of these investments. Is that expensive downtown condo likely to appreciate, or would a cozy suburban home be a better long-term investment? Weighing these factors can help you make decisions that benefit your financial future as a couple.

Lastly, let's talk about preparing for future changes. Life can throw some curveballs—career changes, relocating for a job, or deciding to start a family. Each of these scenarios comes with financial implications. Talk about these possibilities now, even if they seem far off. What would you do if one of you got a dream job offer in another city? How would you handle childcare costs if you decide to have kids? Planning for these changes doesn't mean you have to have all the answers right away, but you're better prepared to handle them as they come. It's about creating a financial strategy that's flexible enough to adapt to whatever life throws your way, ensuring that your finances can keep up as your life changes.

Navigating finances as a couple is a journey of communication, compromise, and joint decision-making. By starting these conversations early, setting clear guidelines and goals, and continuously adapting to life's changes, you and your partner can build a solid financial foundation that supports your relationship through all its phases. Remember, when it comes to money and relationships, the key is to work together, respect each other's perspectives, and keep the lines of communication open. With these strategies, you can turn financial planning from a potential stressor into an opportunity to grow closer and build a prosperous future together.

4.4 PLANNING FOR FINANCIAL EMERGENCIES

Ah, financial emergencies. They're like uninvited guests at your meticulously planned party, popping up just when you've got everything else under control. Whether it's a car that decides to break down at the worst possible time, a medical emergency, or even a sudden job loss, life has its ways of testing your financial resilience. But fear not! With an adaptable emergency fund and a solid action plan, you can tackle these unexpected challenges without breaking a sweat (or the bank).

So, let's talk about your emergency fund. This differs from your regular savings account, where you stash cash for a new phone or a vacation. Think of it as your financial fire extinguisher to douse flames, not for everyday use. The size of this fund should reflect your life stage and responsibilities. Are you just starting your career? Aim for three months' worth of living expenses. Have you got a family or a mortgage? You should bump that up to six months or more. The key here is adaptability. As your life changes—maybe you get a raise, add a family member, or buy a house—so should your emergency fund. Regularly review your living expenses and adjust your fund accordingly. It's like updating your wardrobe: what worked for you a year ago might not fit your needs now.

Having a robust fund is excellent, but it's equally important to keep it accessible. You don't want your money tied up in long-term investments when the car's on the fritz. High-yield savings accounts strike a nice balance between earning interest and providing quick access. These accounts keep your funds liquid (easily convertible to cash), and many come with no or low withdrawal penalties. And let's be honest: in a pinch, the last thing you want is to be penalized for accessing your money.

Let's not forget the importance of a "financial emergency" action plan. This isn't just about having money set aside; it's about knowing exactly what to do when financial storms hit. List potential emergencies—medical issues, home repairs, job loss—and then brainstorm realistic solutions for each. Who would you contact in case of a medical emergency? What's your backup plan if you lose your job? A list of steps can turn panic into action, giving you a clear path forward during stressful times. Think of it as having a map in your glove compartment. Sure, you might have GPS, but something is reassuring about having a physical map when you're lost.

When crafting your emergency action plan, please look at the available resources. Are there family members who could offer support? Do you have insurance policies in place that could mitigate costs? Understanding the resources you can tap into can make all the difference. Also, keep a list of essential contacts—doctors, insurance agents, and your bank's hotline—that are easily accessible. In times of crisis, you won't have the capacity to sift through files or search online. Make it easy on yourself by preparing in advance.

Navigating financial emergencies requires more than just luck: preparation, adaptability, and a cool head. By sizing and maintaining an adequate emergency fund, ensuring quick liquidity, and having a clear, actionable emergency plan, you're not just preparing to manage crises—you're securing your financial well-being against life's inevitable surprises. And while we can't predict every curveball life throws, we can certainly prepare to catch them. So, gear up, plan, and transform those potential disasters into mere bumps in the road.

4.5 JOB LOSS: MANAGING FINANCES DURING UNEMPLOYMENT

So, let's say you've hit a bump in the road—a big one called job loss. It's like someone's pulled the rug out from under you and stings emotionally and financially. Let's put those panic buttons back in the drawer and focus on getting your financial house in order, even if the income part is shaky. Prepping for possible unemployment isn't about being pessimistic; it's about being proactive. Think of it as having a life vest under your seat—it's there if you need it, and boy, will you be glad about it if you do!

First things first: beef up that emergency fund. It's your financial backup parachute. A solid cash reserve can allow you to be selective in your job search rather than grabbing the first thing to pay the rent. Aim to stash away at least three to six months' living expenses. If that sounds like climbing Everest in flip-flops, start small. Even a little buffer is better than none. And while you're still employed, this is the time to cut down on unnecessary expenses—do you need to order takeout five times a week, or could you become the next MasterChef at home?

Now, let's talk about the elephant in the room—debt. Those monthly debt payments might not seem daunting when you've got a regular paycheck. But they can turn into monsters when your income is chopped. If you sense a job loss might be on the horizon, start tackling high-interest debts like credit card balances. Consider shifting them to a lower interest rate option or negotiating with your creditors for better terms. Less debt means fewer worries when you're in a financial tightrope without a safety net.

Alright, so the worst has happened: you've lost your job. It's time to tighten the belt, but there's no need to go to extremes. Start with a survival budget. Trim the fat where you can—goodbye, daily lattes and hello, homemade brews. But keep the essentials intact. Having a functioning phone and internet to job hunt like a boss would be best. And speaking of job hunting, ensure you get all the benefits you're entitled to. Unemployment benefits can be a lifesaver during this time. Get on it fast because sometimes, the processing can take longer than expected.

While you're watching the expenses, let's not forget about making some money too. Enter the world of freelancing and side gigs. Use your existing skills to freelance online or check out gig economy jobs that can fit your schedule. Whether graphic design, tutoring, or dog walking, these gigs can add a bit of padding to your dwindling bank account. Plus, they can be a great way to network and build new skills that might lead to your next full-time job.

Speaking of which, returning to the workforce isn't just about firing off applications. It's also about staying sharp and connected. Invest time updating your skills—online courses can often be done on a shoestring budget and significantly boost your employability. Networking is your best friend here. Reach out to old colleagues, attend industry meetups, and maybe spruce up that LinkedIn profile. Remember, it's not just what you know but who you know. In today's job market, a recommendation from a former coworker or a good word from a professional acquaintance can make all the difference.

So, while losing your job might feel like a plot twist you didn't see coming, it doesn't have to be the end of your financial stability. You can weather this storm with a robust emergency fund, a handle on your debts, and a good strategy for saving on essentials and making extra cash. Keep your head up, your budget tight, and your network active. Opportunities are out there, and with the proper preparation and mindset, you'll be ready to grab them as soon as they appear. Let's turn this temporary setback into a setup for a remarkable comeback!

4.6 RELOCATING: BUDGETING FOR A BIG MOVE

Ah, you are moving! It's like starting a new level in your favorite video game, except the challenges are packing boxes, hauling furniture, and not blowing your budget on takeout because your kitchen is in disarray. Whether you're moving for a new job, school, or just a change of scenery, getting a handle on the costs upfront can save you from the 'why did I do this to myself' financial blues later. Let's unpack (pun intended) how to master the art of moving without letting your bank account take too hard a hit.

First things first, let's estimate those moving costs. It's about more than hiring movers or renting a truck; many hidden expenses can creep up faster than asking your mom why you have yet to unpack. Start by making a list of all anticipated costs—renting moving equipment, buying packing supplies, and, yes, those last-minute runs to the store because you forgot cleaning supplies. Don't forget the security deposits for your new apartment, setup fees for utilities, and any necessary first-time fees that can be easily overlooked. To avoid surprises, add a buffer of around 10-15% to your moving budget for unexpected expenses—because something always comes up.

Now, about those moving supplies. You don't have to buy brand-new boxes—check out local stores or online marketplaces for people giving away boxes and packing materials left over from their moves. This can cut down on costs significantly. And when it comes to hiring movers, get quotes from multiple companies. Don't just look at price—check reviews and ask for recommendations to ensure you're getting reliable service worth your hard-earned dough.

Adjusting to a new cost of living can be like switching from an arcade to a strategy game—suddenly, you need a whole new set of tactics. If you're moving to a city with higher living costs, your everyday expenses like groceries, transportation, and dining out can add up a lot faster than they used to. Before you move, do some research. Sites like Numbeo can compare the cost of living and your current and future cities. Once you have an idea of the differences, start tweaking your budget. Maybe you allocate more to dining and less to transportation if you're moving somewhere with excellent public transit but pricey restaurants.

Minimizing financial stress during the move is all about timing and preparation. Could you plan your move during off-peak times? Most people move at the beginning or the end of the month so that movers might offer better rates in the middle of the month. Selling items you no longer need lightens your load and pads your wallet. Use online platforms or a good old-fashioned garage sale to turn unwanted items into cash. Also, important documents like rental agreements, receipts, and job contracts should be organized and accessible. You'll need these documents to set up new accounts or handle rental contracts.

Establishing financial stability in your new digs after the move is crucial. Start by setting up your banking services. If your current bank doesn't operate in your new area, look for a new bank with better benefits or lower fees. Adjust your budget based on your new living costs and stick to it as you adapt to your new financial environment. Get involved in your new community; understanding local shopping options, entertainment venues, and public transportation can help you find budget-friendly alternatives.

As we wrap up this chapter on navigating life changes and financial decisions, whether you're gearing up for a big move, adjusting post-graduation plans, or merging finances with a partner, remember that these transitions are not just challenges but opportunities. Opportunities to grow, learn, and better prepare for whatever comes next. With the right strategies and a proactive mindset, you can manage and thrive through these changes. Next, we'll dive into more advanced financial planning strategies that will help you continue building on the solid foundation you're setting now. So keep this momentum going, and let's keep turning those financial goals into achievements.

Money Mastery for Young Adults Made Easy
by Ron Martin, CPA

Let's talk about saving money, and no, not in the way where you stash every penny under your mattress and live off ramen noodles (unless you really love ramen, then more power to you). Saving is all about setting yourself up for financial success, both now and in the future. It's like building a safety net that grows bigger every time you add to it. Think of it as paying your future self for all your hard work today.

One of the golden rules of saving is "paying yourself first." It's a simple but powerful concept: before you pay your bills, buy groceries, or spend money on entertainment, you set aside a portion of your income for your savings. It's treating your savings account like another bill that must be paid, ensuring that saving money becomes a regular part of your monthly budget. This approach shifts your mindset from saving what is left over at the end of the month (which, let's be honest, might be nothing) to making saving a priority.

* * *

Make a Difference with Your Review
Unlock the Power of Generosity

The best way to find yourself is to lose yourself in the service of others.

— MAHATMA GANDHI

People who give without expectation live longer, happier lives and make more money. So, if we've got a shot at that during our time together, darn it, I'm going to try.

To make that happen, I have a question for you...

Would you help someone you've never met, even if you never got credit for it?

Who is this person you ask? They are like you. Or, at least, like you used to be. Less experienced, wanting to make a difference, and needing help, but still trying to figure out where to look.

Our mission is to make personal finance for young adults accessible to everyone. Everything we do stems from that mission, and the only way for us to accomplish it is by reaching…well...everyone.

This is where you come in. Most people judge a book by its cover (and its reviews). So, here's my ask on behalf of a struggling young adult you've never met:

Please help that young adult by leaving this book a review.

Your gift costs no money and takes less than 60 seconds to make real, but it can change a fellow young adult's life forever. Your review could help…

...one more small business to provide for their community.
...one more entrepreneur to support their family.
...one more employee to get meaningful work.
…one more client to transform their life.
....one more dream come true.

To get that 'feel good' feeling and help this person for real, all you have to do is...and it takes less than 60 seconds...leave a review.

Scan the QR code or visit the link below to leave your review:

https://www.amazon.com/review/review-your-purchases/?asin=B0DBM14Y9H

If you feel good about helping a faceless young adult, you are my kind of person. Welcome to the club. You're one of us.

I'm much more excited to help you achieve financial confidence, reduce debt, and invest wisely and more efficiently than you can imagine. You'll love the strategies I'm about to share in the coming chapters.

Thank you from the bottom of my heart. Now, back to our regularly scheduled programming.

- Your biggest fan, Ron Martin, CPA

PS - Fun fact: If you provide something of value to another person, it makes you more valuable to them. If you'd like goodwill straight from another young adult - and believe this book will help them - send it their way.

CHAPTER 5
ADVANCED BUDGETING AND SAVING STRATEGIES

ADVANCED BUDGETIING

I magine you're a chef in your financial kitchen. For example, in cooking, where you might experiment with different recipes to find out what tickles your taste buds, budgeting isn't one-size-fits-all. It's about mixing, tasting, and sometimes spicing things up to discover the best budgeting recipe for your financial palate. Whether you're a meticulous planner or a free spirit regarding money, understanding and utilizing the right budgeting strategies can transform how you handle your dough (pun intended). So, let's roll up our sleeves and get into the nitty-gritty of two popular budgeting models: Zero-Based and the 50/30/20 strategy. It's time to find out which financial flavors suit you best!

5.1 ZERO-BASED VS. 50/30/20 BUDGETING MODELS

Zero-Based Budgeting: Every Dollar Has a Job

First up is the Zero-Based budgeting model, also known as the "give every dollar a job" approach. Imagine you're doling out tasks to your expenses as if you're the boss at a money management firm. The goal here is to allocate every single dollar of your income to specific costs, savings, and debt payments, ensuring that your income minus your expenditures equals zero by the end of the month. It's like planning a dinner party where you assign every piece of cutlery its role—nothing is left wandering around the drawer.

This method is stellar for those who need a firm handle on where every penny is going. It forces you to think about how you spend each dollar, making it harder for random, impulsive purchases to sneak past your budget. However, it does require a bit more time and vigilance. You'll be tracking every transaction, which can be as detailed as it sounds, but it's worth it if it means getting your finances into shipshape.

50/30/20 Budgeting: Simplicity in Three Acts

On the other side of the budgeting spectrum, we have the 50/30/20 rule, a beautifully simple and somewhat more flexible strategy. Here's how it breaks down: 50% of your income goes to necessities (rent, utilities, and groceries), 30% to wants (like that trendy new restaurant or the latest smartphone), and the remaining 20% slides into savings and debt repayment. It's like dividing your plate at a buffet—one part greens, one part proteins, and a little space for that delicious dessert.

The 50/30/20 method is perfect for those who want a less detailed framework that still provides structure and accountability. It offers a good balance, ensuring you cover essential expenses and savings without making you account for every last cent. Plus, it gives you the flexibility to enjoy life's luxuries, which we all need a bit of spice in our financial lives!

What do you think works best for you?

Choosing between these two models depends mainly on your financial situation and temperament. If you're someone who loves detail and enjoys being in control of every financial aspect, zero-based budgeting might be your soulmate. But if you prefer a broader overview and less micromanagement, the 50/30/20 approach could be your perfect match.

Real-Life in Action: Case Studies

Let's see these models in action. Take Jamie, for example, a freelancer whose income varies monthly. Jamie finds zero-based budgeting ideal because it allows her to allocate funds based on fluctuating income, ensuring she's covered for essentials and knows exactly where her money goes each month. On the flip side, there's Alex, a school teacher with a stable income, who loves the 50/30/20 method because it simplifies her finances and still allows room for weekend getaways and hobbies.

Both budgeting models have their perks and can be highly effective —it comes down to personal preference and financial goals. Whether you're a meticulous planner or like a bit of flexibility, the key is consistency. Stick with your chosen method, adjust as needed, and watch as your financial control and confidence soar. Remember, budgeting isn't about restricting your life but empowering it. So, choose the suitable method, and start mixing up the perfect financial recipe for your life!

5.2 AUTOMATING YOUR SAVINGS: SET IT AND FORGET IT

Could you consider the last time you tried to keep a plant alive? You might have the best intentions to water it regularly, but life gets busy, and before you know it, you're holding a mini funeral for your fern. Saving money can be like that—good intentions, but sometimes, not the best follow-through. That's where automating your savings comes into play. It's like setting up a drip irrigation system for your finances, ensuring your savings grow consistently without needing to remember to water them daily.

Setting up automatic savings is like putting your financial growth on autopilot. Most banks and many apps now offer the option to automate transfers from your checking account to your savings account. You decide how much and how often—maybe a small amount every week or a chunk of change monthly, right after payday. This way, the money is whisked away before you consider spending it on another impulse buy. It's about making your laziness work in your favor; by setting things up once, you're saving yourself from having to make the same decision to save repeatedly.

The trick is to start small, especially if you're nervous about overcommitting. Automating $5 or $10 per paycheck can build up over time. Then, as you adjust to your budget, you can increase the amount gradually. Some folks like to sync their savings with their pay cycle so the money is out of sight before they can spend it. Others set it up around big bills, ensuring they don't accidentally overspend right before rent is due. The key is consistency, and by automating, you're locking down that consistency without any extra effort.

Psychological Benefits of "Set It and Forget It"

Now, let's talk about the mental magic of automating your savings. Have you ever heard of 'out of sight, out of mind'? That's precisely what makes automation so powerful. Moving money directly into savings makes you less likely to consider it available for spending. It's a psychological trick that helps reduce the temptation to splurge, making saving feel less like a daily struggle and more like a natural part of your financial routine. Over time, this can help build a 'savings habit,' reinforcing the idea that you save regularly, which can be incredibly empowering.

Regularly seeing your savings grow without additional effort can be a huge motivational boost. It's like watching your fitness progress after weeks of workouts. Every time you check your savings balance and see it a little higher, it's a reminder that you're moving closer to your financial goals, whether that's a dream vacation, a new car, or just the security of a robust emergency fund.

Tools and Apps to Make It Even Easier

Thankfully, we're living in the golden age of financial technology, and tons of tools are designed to make saving as painless as possible. Apps like Oportun analyze your spending habits and automatically transfer small amounts of money from checking to savings based on what you can afford at any given time. It's like having an intelligent assistant who constantly watches over your finances, ensuring you save optimally without disrupting your daily life.

Another great option is Qapital, which allows you to set specific savings goals and rules for when and how you save. You can round up your change to the nearest dollar on every purchase and save the difference, or you can set it to transfer a certain amount every time you indulge in a guilty pleasure like ordering takeout. It makes saving feel like a fun game where your points are dollars in your bank account.

Most traditional banks offer automated transfers you can set up through their online banking portals for those who like a more straightforward approach. This might have different bells and whistles of some apps. Still, it's a solid, reliable way to ensure your money consistently flows into your savings without any manual input you need after the initial setup.

So, whether you're a tech-savvy saver looking for the latest app or prefer the traditional banking approach, the tools are out there. By taking advantage of these technologies, you're not just making saving easier; you're ensuring it happens. As your savings grow, every automated transfer reinforces that you're taking concrete steps toward a more secure financial future without lifting a finger after the initial setup. Isn't technology incredible?

5.3 HACK YOUR SAVINGS: TIPS FOR BIGGER GROWTH

So, you're already on your way to becoming a savvy saver, but maybe you're itching to turbo-charge your savings game even more. Well, buckle up because we're about to shift into high gear with some excellent strategies to make your money grow faster and work harder. Consider upgrading from a bike to a motorcycle in your savings journey. Let's zoom into how high-yield savings accounts, certificates of deposit (CDs), cash-back programs, and some pretty nifty unconventional hacks can rev up your financial engine.

High-Yield Savings Accounts: Your Money's Best Friend

First off, let's chat about high-yield savings accounts. If you're still stashing your savings in a regular account, you're letting your money take a long nap. High-yield savings accounts wake that money up by offering higher interest rates—think of it as your money getting a job and earning you more cash without you lifting a finger. These accounts are like the unsung heroes of the banking world; they're easy to set up, super safe, and your cash is always there when needed. Plus, they're perfect for your emergency fund or saving for big goals like a dream vacation or a down payment on a condo. By switching to a high-yield account, you can see your savings grow significantly faster, thanks to those higher interest rates. It's like feeding your money a performance-enhancing diet—it works harder.

Certificates of Deposit (CDs): The Tortoise in the Race

CDs can be a great way to boost your savings if you've got some cash you won't need for a while. Think of CDs as a timed savings account. You agree to leave your money in the bank for a set period, like one year, three years, or even longer, and in exchange, the bank agrees to pay you more interest than you'd get from a regular savings or high-yield account. It's like putting your dollars into hibernation; they sleep for a while and wake up more enormous thanks to the magic of higher fixed interest rates. Please remember patience is the key here. Pulling out your money early can hit you with penalties, so only lock away cash you will need once the term ends. For those who like a bit more flexibility, consider laddering your CDs. This strategy involves having multiple CDs that mature at different times, providing you regular access to parts of your cash while enjoying higher interest rate benefits. Sites like Bankrate allow you to find the best high-yield accounts and CD rates.

Cash-Back and Rewards Programs: The Fun Way to Save

Let's move on to something a bit more fun—cash-back and rewards programs. If you're going to spend money, you might as well get some of it back, right? Using a cash-back credit card for your purchases can be a game-changer. Whether it's groceries, gas, or even your morning coffee, you can earn back a percentage of your spending. It's like having a little savings booster on everything you buy. But here's the key: you have to pay off that card in full every month to benefit. Letting balances carry over and paying interest would eat up all those lovely cash-back gains. For extra savings, stack your credit card rewards with cash-back apps and websites that offer rebates or special deals when shopping online or in-store. It's like double-dipping your chips in the savings salsa. Sites like Nerdwallet let you shop for the best credit card rewards programs.

Unconventional Saving Hacks: Think Outside the Bank

Finally, let's get a bit creative with some unconventional saving hacks. Have you ever thought about renting out your stuff? Platforms like Fat Llama let you rent out almost anything—your camera, bike, even your drone. It's a great way to make your possessions earn their keep. Or how about digitizing your spare change? Apps like Acorns round up your transactions to the nearest dollar and invest the difference. It's painless, and you'll be amazed how quickly those pennies can turn into dollars.

5.4 SEASONAL BUDGET ADJUSTMENTS: PLANNING FOR HOLIDAYS AND VACATIONS

Ah, the joys of the holiday season and the adventures of vacation planning—times of cheer, relaxation, and often a hefty dose of financial stress. It's no secret that your wallet can feel significantly lighter during these festive or travel-heavy periods. The key to not letting seasonal splurges turn into financial frostbite is all in the planning. Think of it as preparing for a big game or a marathon—you wouldn't just wing it, right? The same goes for managing your money during high-spending seasons.

Let's break it down: during the holidays, expenses can skyrocket faster than a firework on the Fourth of July. Gifts, decorations, parties, and travel can drain your bank account if you're not careful. And vacations? While they're fantastic for your Instagram feed and mental health, they can wreak havoc on your finances if not thoughtfully budgeted for. This is where seasonal budgeting swoops in to save the day. By adjusting your budget to account for these expected increases in spending, you can enjoy the season's festivities or that dream trip without the lingering hangover of debt.

Strategizing Your Seasonal Savings Plan

Creating a seasonal savings plan starts months in advance. Just like squirrels stash away nuts for the winter, you'll want to start setting aside money well before the holiday decorations hit the shelves or you start packing your bags. One effective strategy is to estimate your total expected expenses for these periods and then break that down into manageable monthly savings goals. For instance, if you anticipate needing an extra $600 for holiday expenses in June, setting aside $100 a month gets you there stress-free by December.

Automating this savings process can make it even easier. Set up a separate savings account for holidays and vacations, and schedule automatic transfers that align with your paydays. This way, the money is out of sight and out of mind, earmarked for fun and festivities, reducing the temptation to dip into it for other expenses.

Minimizing Seasonal Expenses: Smart and Creative Tips

Now, saving for these seasons is excellent, but minimizing expenses during them? Even better. Consider traveling during the off-season or mid-week when flights and hotels are often cheaper. Not only do you save money, but you also avoid the crowds—a win-win! Homemade gifts or experiences can be much more meaningful (and budget-friendly) than pricey store-bought holiday items. Organize potluck holiday dinners instead of hosting a lavish feast all by yourself. This cuts costs and adds variety and fun as everyone brings something to the table.

For vacations, leverage travel reward programs. Using points or miles for flights, hotels, or rental cars can significantly reduce travel costs. Look for deals and discounts, and always compare prices across multiple platforms before booking. Remember, a little research goes a long way in stretching your vacation dollars.

Real-Life Victories: Celebrating Smart Spending

Consider the case of Lisa and Mark, a couple who loves to travel but hates the stress of holiday debt. They start their vacation fund at the beginning of each year, setting aside a portion of their monthly income. By the time their vacation rolls around, they've got enough saved to cover all their expenses without touching their credit cards. They also watch for airline ticket sales and book their accommodations through platforms offering the best deals without compromising comfort or location. Two examples are Priceline and Expedia.

Then there's Jenna, who thrives during the holiday season by crafting personalized gifts and organizing group gift exchanges, significantly reducing her spending. She hosts a DIY decorations night, turning it into a fun activity with friends, saving money, and creating cherished memories.

These stories highlight effective planning and creative spending strategies for enjoyable seasons without financial strain. By adopting similar approaches, you can transform what might typically be a wallet-draining period into a well-budgeted, stress-free experience. Whether through savvy saving tactics, smart spending, or a combination of both, mastering seasonal budget adjustments ensures you can fully engage in the joy of holidays and vacations without the burden of financial woes.

5.5 COUPONING AND DISCOUNT SHOPPING IN THE DIGITAL AGE

Let's be honest: who doesn't love scoring a sweet deal? It's like finding an extra fry at the bottom of your takeout bag—unexpected and extraordinary. Welcome to the digital couponing and discount shopping world, where saving money on groceries, clothing, and other essentials is not just bright—it's an art form. With the rise of technology, clipping physical coupons has morphed into tapping apps and browsing websites offering a treasure trove of discounts at your fingertips. Let's dive into how you can master this modern money-saving craft.

First up, digital coupons are your new best friends. They are magic wands that slash prices with a single tap or click. These little digital wonders are available through apps or websites, and they can significantly cut down your spending on daily essentials. For groceries, apps like Ibotta and Checkout 51 are game changers. They offer cash back on select items when you upload a receipt proving your purchase. For general shopping, Rakuten, RetailMeNot, Capital One Shopping, and Honey automatically apply the best coupon codes at checkout, ensuring you never miss out on a deal. It's like having a personal assistant to find you the best price minus the hefty salary.

Now, while diving into the digital coupon pool can be thrilling, it's easy to get carried away. Here's where strategy plays a crucial role. Start by setting clear shopping goals. What do you need, and what's just nice to have? Once you've got your list, it's time to match coupons with upcoming sales. Many stores release their promotional cycles in advance, allowing you to stack coupons on top of sale prices for double the savings. Imagine buying that fancy shampoo at half price and then knocking off another couple of bucks with a coupon—suddenly, it's not just shampoo; it's a steal.

However, as with all good things, there's a catch. One of the most common pitfalls in digital couponing is buying stuff you don't need just because there's a discount. Retailers are savvy at tempting shoppers with eye-catching deals that might not be as beneficial as they seem. Always ask yourself: would I buy this if it weren't on sale? If the answer is no, it's probably best to leave it. Remember, a great deal isn't great if it's for something you won't use. It's like buying a ticket for a rollercoaster you have no intention of riding—exciting but ultimately pointless.

Tools and apps are your navigational aids when navigating the digital discount landscape. Apps like Flipp can pull digital flyers from your local stores, allowing you to compare prices and efficiently plan your shopping trips. For online shopping, browser extensions like Cently can automatically search the Internet for discount codes when you check out, ensuring you always get the best possible deal without having to hunt for codes yourself. These tools save you money and time, making the shopping experience less about stress and more about success.

So, as you tap into digital couponing and discount shopping, remember that the goal is to make your life easier and your expenses lighter. With some strategy, restraint, and the right technological tools, you can transform how you shop, turning every transaction into a triumph. Whether stocking up on pantry staples or splurging on that new outfit, mastering the art of digital savings is a skill that pays off—literally. So embrace the digital age of couponing and watch as your savings stack up, one clever swipe at a time.

5.6 SIDE HUSTLES: BALANCING TIME AND MONEY

So, you're thinking about jumping into the world of side hustles? Welcome to the ultimate multitasking challenge, where you balance time, money, and probably a bit of sanity. Side hustles are like that extra spice you add to your financial recipe—they can kick things up a notch, especially when your primary income feels more like a steady simmer than a full boil. But as with any good dish, the key is balancing the ingredients. Too much can overwhelm you, and too little might not make the impact you're hoping for.

Let's break down the real deal about side hustles. They're not just a quick cash grab; they require real-time and energy commitments. Think of them as mini-jobs; they come with their own set of responsibilities and rewards. For instance, freelancing might offer flexible hours and potentially lucrative pay, but it can also demand irregular working times and client management, which might not be everyone's cup of tea. Conversely, something more structured, like driving for a ride-share service, can offer more predictable hours but often for less pay. The trick is to weigh the potential earnings against your investment time. It's about finding that sweet spot where your time is worth the financial output.

Now, let's talk about variety because the world of side hustles is as varied as your playlist. From freelance graphic design and writing to dog walking or tutoring, there's a side gig to match almost any skill and schedule. If you're a night owl, how about freelance writing or coding? Morning person? Perhaps a couple of hours as a fitness trainer at a local café or a morning gym session. The key is aligning your side hustle with your strengths and lifestyle. This alignment not only makes the work more enjoyable but also more sustainable in the long run.

Managing your time effectively is crucial, particularly if you're juggling this side hustle with a full-time job or studies. It's like being a DJ at a complex mixing board; you've got to keep all the levels right to make sure the sound is perfect. Tools like Google Calendar or Trello can help you visually organize your tasks and time. Setting specific work hours for your side hustle and sticking to them can help categorize your responsibilities, ensuring your side gig doesn't bleed into your personal life or principal job. Also, don't underestimate the power of saying no. Taking on more than you can handle can quickly turn your side hustle from a dream into a nightmare.

Success in the side hustle game is not just about making extra cash; it's about creating opportunities and learning new skills that can pay off. Take Sarah, for instance, who started a small weekend gig as a wedding photographer. What began as a way to make extra money became a full-time business once she realized how much she loved and excelled at photography. Or consider Mike, who turned his love for tutoring into a thriving online math coaching service, all while keeping his day job as an engineer. Both found ways to align their passions with opportunities that provided extra income, personal growth, and satisfaction.

In wrapping up this dive into the world of side hustles, remember it's all about balance. Choosing the right hustle, aligning it with your lifestyle, managing your time wisely, and always being ready to learn from the experience are critical to surviving and thriving in your extra work. Whether padding your wallet, exploring a passion, or expanding your skill set, a side hustle can be a powerful addition to your financial strategy if you play your cards right. So gear up, get out there, and start hustling smart!

As we close this chapter on advanced budgeting and saving strategies, you're now equipped with the insights and tools to manage your money more effectively and make it grow. From mastering dynamic budgeting methods to automating your savings and even turning hobbies into profitable side hustles, you have what it takes to take your financial game to the next level. Ready for more? Next up, we'll explore the intricacies of credit management and investment strategies that can further enhance your financial landscape. Stay tuned; the journey to financial mastery continues!

CHAPTER 6
CREDIT MASTERY AND AVOIDING PITFALLS

Alright, let's talk credit. Think of credit like your financial GPA—it shows how well you handle your money, and trust me, you want to keep those scores high. But what if you're starting from scratch? No worries, I've got you covered. We're going to turn you into a credit-building ninja, even if you're currently a blank slate in the eyes of credit bureaus. Let's dive into the ABCs of starting your credit journey, securing your financial reputation one smart move at a time.

6.1 BUILDING YOUR CREDIT FROM SCRATCH

Start with Secured Credit Products

Imagine trying to prove to a friend that you can handle a pet. But instead of starting with a high-maintenance puppy, you kick things off with a low-risk goldfish. That's the idea behind secured credit products. Secured credit cards and builder loans are like training wheels for your credit score. They're designed for credit newbies—people who banks look at and say, "Um, who are you again?"

With a secured credit card, you make a cash deposit that becomes your credit limit. This way, the bank feels safe, and you can practice using credit without the risk of going overboard. It's a win-win. You use the card for a few routine expenses, pay off the balance each month, and just like that, you're building credit. Builder loans work similarly; the lender holds the loan amount while you make payments, which gets reported to credit bureaus. In the end, not only do you have a better credit score, but you also get your loan amount back. Pretty neat, right?

The Role of Co-signers

Let's say you want to speed up the process or get a bigger loan or an unsecured credit card, but your credit is still more invisible than your socks in the laundry. Here's where a co-signer comes in handy. A co-signer with a good credit score agrees to back up your loan. Think of them like a wingman who helps you score credibility points.

However, it's not all high-fives and easy sailing. Co-signing is a big deal. If you mess up, miss payments, or default, your co-signer's credit gets dinged, and they're on the hook for the debt. And yes, it can make Thanksgiving dinner awkward if you let things go south. So, if you go this route, ensure you're as committed to keeping up with payments as you are to binge-watching your favorite series.

Importance of Utility and Rent Payments

Paying for the roof over your head and keeping the lights on doesn't just keep you comfortable—it can also build your credit. More and more, rent and utility payments are recognized in credit reports. Services like Experian Boost allow you to add these payments to your credit history. It's like getting financial brownie points for paying bills you're already covering. Make sure you're consistently on time with these payments because, while they can boost your score, missed payments can also take a hit on your credit.

Timeline of Credit Score Development

So, how long does all this credit-building magic take? Well, it's not instantaneous (I wish!). Think of it as growing a plant—from seedling to full bloom- and it takes patience and consistent care. Typically, generating a credit score from scratch can take about three to six months of regular credit activity. But remember, building a solid score can take years of good habits. Keep your credit utilization low (that's how much credit you use compared to how much you have), always pay on time, and don't go wild opening new accounts too often.

Building credit from scratch is like learning a new dance. It might feel awkward at first, and you might step on a few toes, but you'll move confidently with practice. Just stick with it, keep it responsible, and before you know it, you'll have lenders and creditors lining up at your door, scores in hand, ready to give you the financial respect you've earned. Keep at it, and let's make your credit score something to brag about!

6.2 REPAIRING BAD CREDIT: A RECOVERABLE JOURNEY

Imagine you've had a bit of a wild ride with your finances, and now your credit score looks more like a bad weather report—stormy with a chance of more turmoil. But don't worry; cleaning up your credit isn't as daunting as it sounds. It's like tidying up after a big party; it takes effort and the right tools, but it's doable. Let's roll up our sleeves and get your credit score back in shape, showing you exactly how to spot errors, negotiate like a pro, and decide if a credit repair service is worth the dough.

Step-by-Step Guide to Disputing Credit Report Errors

First things first, you'll need a copy of your credit report. You're entitled to a free report from each of the three major bureaus—Equifax, Experian, and TransUnion—once a year through AnnualCreditReport.com. This is like getting a snapshot of your financial reputation. Scrutinize this report as if you're looking for where your roommate hid your favorite snacks. Look for any mistakes, like payments marked late when you paid on time or, even worse, accounts that aren't even yours.

Found an error? It's time to channel your inner lawyer and dispute it. You'll need to write a dispute letter to the credit bureau, saying, "Hey, this info isn't right; please fix it." Include copies (never originals) of documents supporting your case, like bank statements or payment confirmations. The bureau then has 30 days to investigate and respond. If they agree with you, they'll fix your report, and your credit score gets a boost just like that.

Negotiating with Creditors

If your credit report is accurate but shows legit blemishes, like when you paid your credit card bill as late as a lousy wizard, it's time to talk to your creditors. Think of it as negotiating a peace treaty. Reach out and be honest about your financial situation. You might be surprised how willing they are to work with you. Ask for lower interest rates or see if they'll accept a smaller payment if you pay a lump sum. Just remember, get any agreement in writing. It's your financial safety net to ensure they stick to the deal.

Sometimes, settling for less than what you owe can be a viable strategy, especially if it's a choice between that and not paying. This means you'll likely take a hit on your credit score in the short term, but clearing the debt can provide a clean slate to rebuild.

Credit Repair Services: Are They Worth It?

Now, what if you're thinking about bringing in the pros? Credit repair services can seem like a shiny knight ready to rescue your credit score, but they're not all created equal. Some are incredibly helpful, guiding you through the process and handling disputes on your behalf. Others? Not so much. They might promise the world but deliver nothing more than a lighter wallet. If you decide to go this route, do your homework. Review reviews, look for complaints with the Better Business Bureau, and read the fine print before signing up.

Please be careful of any service that asks for money upfront or promises a quick fix. Authentic credit repair takes time—like slow-cooking a good stew. It's about consistent effort and innovative financial behavior over time.

Success Stories of Credit Recovery

Sometimes, hearing that others have successfully navigated out of credit chaos can be just the motivation you need. Take Sarah, for example. She racked up a hefty credit card balance in college, thinking her future self would somehow handle it. Fast forward a few years, and her credit score was napping on the ocean floor. But by using a combination of disputing inaccuracies and negotiating lower interest rates, she managed to get her credit score back to respectability—and now she's even been approved for a mortgage.

Then there's Mike. He missed several payments on his car loan when he lost his job, and his credit score was about as healthy as a plant you forgot to water for a month. Mike worked with a credit counseling service, which helped him consolidate his debts and negotiate a manageable payment plan with creditors. A few years later, his credit score is better than ever, and he's teaching his kids how early financial responsibility can save a lot of stress later on.

These stories aren't just feel-good moments; they're proof that repairing bad credit isn't just possible with the right approach—it's achievable. Whether you tackle it yourself or get help, the path to a better credit score is worth taking. So grab your financial toolkit, and let's get to work. Your credit score is ready to rise; you're just the person to lift it.

6.3 UNDERSTANDING AND USING CREDIT WISELY

Let's crack the code on using credit wisely because, believe it or not, all credit is not created equal. There are as many types of credit as there are flavors of ice cream, and just like choosing between rocky road and vanilla, the kind of credit you pick can affect how sweet the outcome is. So, whether you're eyeing a personal loan for a big-ticket purchase, swiping your credit card for groceries, or considering a line of credit for unexpected expenses, understanding what can help you use credit to your advantage without getting a financial brain freeze.

Different Types of Credit: A Quick Tour

First, there's the straightforward personal loan. Consider this as borrowing a lump sum for specific needs like consolidating debt or funding an alien-themed wedding. You get the money upfront and pay it back with interest over a predetermined period. It's simple and predictable, which is excellent for budgeting. Then there are credit cards—your go-to for everyday purchases, emergency costs, or just earning rewards. They're super flexible but can be slippery if not managed wisely due to high interest rates and tempting credit limits.

Next are lines of credit, like having a magic pot that refills as you pay it back. You have a set credit limit, and you can borrow as much as you need up to that limit, making it ideal for ongoing expenses like home renovations or combating alien invasions (hey, you never know). Each of these credit types has its place, but the key is knowing when to use which. Personal loans are excellent for significant, one-time expenses; credit cards are perfect for short-term borrowing, and lines of credit work well for ongoing or uncertain costs.

Good Debt vs. Bad Debt: Decoding the Mystery

Now, let's talk about good debt versus bad debt because there's such a thing as good debt! Good debt is like investing in your future —think of student loans for education that boost your earning potential or a mortgage for a home that is appreciated over time. These kinds of debts can set you up for financial success. Bad debt, on the other hand, includes things that lose value fast or carry high interest rates that make them challenging to pay off—like high-interest credit card debt used for splurging on ultra-luxury alien gear.

Interest Rates and Fees: The Nitty-Gritty

Understanding interest rates and fees can save you money and headaches. Interest rates can be fixed (staying the same throughout the term of your loan) or variable (changing with market conditions). Fixed rates offer stability, while variable rates might save you money if rates go down. However, if rates go up, so do your payments. Then, there are late, over-limit, annual, and more fees. Always read the fine print so you know what you might be charged. This can help you avoid nasty surprises when your bill arrives.

Best Practices for Using Credit Cards

Credit cards are fantastic tools if used right. They can help you build credit, earn rewards, and handle emergencies—all while keeping your cash flow smooth. The golden rule? Always aim to pay off your balance in full each month. This way, you avoid interest charges and keep your credit score healthy. If you can't always do that, keep your balance below 30% of your credit limit. This helps maintain a good credit utilization ratio, positively impacting your credit score.

Using credit cards wisely also means taking advantage of their benefits. Many cards offer rewards like cash back, points, or travel perks. Use these to your advantage by choosing cards that align with your spending habits and goals. For instance, if you travel a lot, a card offering travel rewards and no foreign transaction fees might be perfect.

Credit isn't just a financial tool—it's a way to build your financial future, one wise decision at a time. By understanding the different types of credit, knowing when and how to use them, and managing them wisely, you can turn credit into a lever that lifts your financial well-being. So whether you're booking a trip to Mars or buying groceries, remember these tips and use credit to your advantage. Keep these strategies in mind, and you'll not only keep your finances healthy but also take full advantage of the opportunities that good credit management offers.

6.4 CREDIT MYTHS DEBUNKED

Ah, credit myths! They're like those urban legends everyone at school swore were true until someone finally busted them with facts. Let's clear up some of the most common misconceptions about credit floating around so you can manage your credit like a pro without falling for the myths that trip up so many.

First, let's talk about the fear of checking your credit score. Many folks hesitate to check their scores because they've heard it can drag their score down. Here's the real deal: checking your credit score is considered a "soft inquiry" and doesn't affect your score. It's like checking your reflection in a mirror; it doesn't change how you look; it just shows you what's up. This myth probably comes from confusing it with "hard inquiries," which happen when lenders check your score to decide if they'll lend you money. Those can affect your score, but only slightly. So, feel free to check your score as often as you need to keep informed about your credit health.

Another common myth is that your income influences your credit score. Let's set the record straight: your income doesn't directly impact your credit score. Credit scores are calculated based on your payment history, amounts owed, length of credit history, new credit, and types of credit used—not how much money you make. However, higher income might help you pay off debts more efficiently, which indirectly can help your score. But just because you earn more doesn't mean your credit score automatically goes up.

Finally, let's debunk some misconceptions about closing credit accounts. It might feel like a good idea to cut up your credit cards and close the accounts to improve your credit score, right? Not so fast. Closing credit accounts can hurt your credit score. It reduces your overall available credit, which can increase your credit utilization ratio—a key factor in your credit score. If you close older accounts, it can also shorten your credit history, which can further lower your score. The best approach? Keep your older accounts open, even if you're not using them much, and focus on paying down balances to keep your credit utilization low.

Understanding the facts behind these myths allows you to take control of your credit without unnecessary fears or misconceptions clouding your judgment. Armed with the truth, you can use credit wisely, making decisions that support your financial health and future goals. So the next time someone tells you a spooky credit myth, you'll know better than to take it at face value. Remember these clarifications as you navigate the credit landscape, and you'll be well on your way to becoming a credit-savvy individual. Keep on debunking those myths, and watch your credit confidence soar!

6.5 PROTECTING YOURSELF AGAINST CREDIT FRAUD

Imagine you're having a good time at a party when suddenly you realize someone's rifled through your jacket and snagged your wallet. That sinking feeling? That's akin to discovering you're a victim of credit fraud. But fear not! While the digital age has made our financial lives as easy as scrolling on our smartphones, it has also given rise to a new breed of wallet thieves: cybercriminals. They're sneaky, they're sly, and they're out to snag your financial info. But with the proper knowledge and tools, you can shield yourself like a credit superhero.

Let's start by understanding the rogues' gallery of credit fraud. Identity theft tops the list – it's like someone clones you financially, using your info to open accounts, rack up charges, or take out loans all in your name. Then there's card skimming – ever swiped your card at a gas station or an ATM and later found mysterious charges? That's skimming. Crooks install devices to steal your card data, then go on a shopping spree on your dime. Phishing is another sneaky tactic; have you ever received an email or a message that looked legit asking for your account details? That's a phishing attempt right there, trying to bait you into giving away the keys to your financial kingdom. And let's not forget about online scams, the digital equivalent of a con artist, tricking you into handing over money or data with promises of fake rewards or threats of dire consequences.

Now that you know the enemies, how do you armor up? First, think of your info as a VIP – paramount privacy. Guard it fiercely. When online, ensure you're on secure connections; look for URLs that start with "https" – that 's' stands for secure. Public Wi-Fi might be convenient, but it is also a hacker's playground. Avoid accessing sensitive info like your bank accounts unless you're on a secured network. Regular password changes? Non-negotiable. Make them complex and unique. And just like you wouldn't use a flimsy lock on your front door, don't skimp on your digital security. Use robust antivirus software to keep malware at bay, and consider a Virtual Private Network (VPN) for an extra layer of protection.

But what if, despite your best efforts, you suspect you're dealing with credit fraud? First, don't panic. Swift action can minimize the damage. Start by alerting your bank or credit card issuer. They can freeze your account, stopping the fraudster in their tracks. Next, pull up your credit reports. You're looking for any accounts or transactions you don't recognize. If something looks fishy, it's time to dispute it. Contact the credit bureaus – Equifax, Experian, and TransUnion – and flag the fraudulent activity. They're obliged to investigate and scrub any illegitimate info from your record. Keep a detailed log of your actions and communications; this will be invaluable if things get complicated. And don't forget to file a report with the Federal Trade Commission (FTC) through IdentityTheft.gov. It's the government's way of knuckling down on identity theft, and it helps them keep tabs on what kinds of scams are trending.

All three credit bureaus mentioned above can freeze your credit report for free so that no one can open a credit account in your name. This is good protection to have. If you do this you must freeze all three credit bureaus. You can do this online or you can call them. Here are the websites and contact information.

- Equifax - https://www.equifax.com/personal/credit-report-services/credit-freeze - Phone number 888-298-0045
- Experian - https://www.experian.com Then scroll down to Security Freeze. - Phone number 888-397-3742
- Transunion - https://www.transunion.com/credit-freeze - Phone number 888-916-8800

If you want to open a credit account, such as a credit card or to get a loan, you will need to unfreeze your credit bureau temporarily. Again all three credit bureaus must be done and this is still free to do.

Let's talk about credit monitoring services. These are like having a lookout; they keep an eye on your credit reports and alert you to changes, which could be a sign of foul play. Some services offer additional protection, like identity theft insurance or recovery services, to help you bounce back if your data gets compromised. But before you sign up, weigh the costs against the benefits. Some banks or credit card companies offer monitoring services for free or at a reduced price. Shop around, read the fine print, and decide if the extra protection is worth your investment.

Navigating the murky waters of credit fraud can be daunting, but with the proper knowledge and tools, you can protect your financial identity like a pro. Stay vigilant, stay informed, and don't let the fraudsters get the upper hand. Remember, knowledge isn't just power in personal finance—it's protection.

6.6 CREDIT AND MAJOR PURCHASES: WHAT TO KNOW

When you're gearing up to make those big-ticket purchases like snagging your first ride or diving into homeownership, your credit needs to be in tip-top shape. Think of your credit score as your financial wingman—having it in good standing can make all the difference in snagging those keys confidently. So, how do you prep your credit for these significant moves? First off, buff up that credit score. This means keeping up with your payments and whittling down any high balances. Also, start saving for a solid down payment. This shows lenders you're serious and can also reduce the amount you need to borrow, which is always a plus.

Now, let's talk loans. Securing a mortgage or auto loan isn't just about signing some papers; it's about understanding what lenders are looking for and playing your cards right to get the best rates. Lenders love stability, so having a steady job and a good income history can help your case. They'll comb through your credit report, looking at your debt-to-income ratio—your monthly debt payments divided by your monthly income. Keeping this ratio low shows you aren't biting off more debt than you can chew.

Shopping around for rates can save you a ton of cash in the long run. Don't just go with the first offer. You can check out different lenders for the lowest interest rate. Sometimes, the best deals are found through credit unions or online lenders, so keep your options open. And remember, every percentage point counts when discussing loans that can stretch over several decades.

Taking on a big loan is a significant commitment that can hang over your financial life for years. That's why understanding the long-term implications of substantial debt is crucial. Sure, that shiny new car or beautiful home feels excellent now, but consider the total cost over time. Interest can add up to a hefty sum, turning a reasonable purchase into a financial burden if not managed wisely.

After you've locked down that loan and made the purchase, the real work begins: keeping your financial health in check. It's crucial to manage your finances smartly post-purchase. This means sticking to a budget, saving, and keeping up with loan payments. Late payments can be a significant setback for your credit score. Consider setting up automatic payments to dodge those pitfalls and keep your credit score climbing.

Now, integrating these strategies ensures you secure the purchases you want and maintain a robust financial standing afterward. By preparing your credit, choosing the right loan, understanding the long-term effects of your debt, and managing your finances with an iron fist post-purchase, you set yourself up to survive and thrive in your financial life. Next, we'll dive deeper into more nuanced aspects of personal finance management. Stay tuned, and let's keep those financial wins coming!

CHAPTER 7
TAX ESSENTIALS AND MAXIMIZING YOUR INCOME

Have you ever felt like the world of taxes is a maze designed by a mad scientist specifically to confuse everyone? You're not alone. But fear not because today we'll turn that intimidating tax maze into a walk in the park. Think of this chapter as your GPS through the world of taxes, designed to help you navigate the twists and turns like a pro. Whether dealing with your first tax return or figuring out if you need to bother, I've got your back. Ready to crack the tax code? Let's jump right in!

7.1 BASICS OF TAXES FOR YOUNG ADULTS

The ABCs of Taxes: Federal, State, and Local

First, let's break down the types of taxes you might encounter. Taxes come in three flavors: federal, state, and local. Federal taxes are the big boss, used by the government to fund national things like defense, social security, and many other programs that cover the country. Then you've got state taxes, which can vary wildly depending on where you live. Some states, like Texas and Florida, don't have income tax, which sounds great, but they might get you higher sales or property taxes. Some cities or counties charge local taxes for services like police, schools, and those potholes they keep promising to fix.

Income is taxed in brackets, meaning you pay different rates on different chunks of your money, like layers of a cake. The more you make, the higher the percentage you'll pay on the top layers. It's progressive, so as you climb the income ladder, so does the tax rate on your new "top" dollars.

Who Needs to File and When

Navigating who needs to file taxes can feel like decoding a secret message. Here's the scoop: you probably need to file if you made over a certain amount in a year. This amount can change, but it starts when you earn about $13,850 a year for most single young adults. Filing isn't just about paying what's due; it's also about getting back any excess taxes you've paid through refunds. If you're shooting for tax credits (like for education or being low-income), you'll need to file to claim those benefits.

Deadlines are the dates by which you need to either file your taxes or ask for an extension. Typically, it's April 15th for federal taxes. Missing this date without an extension could mean you could be looking at penalties. It's like RSVPing late to a wedding and finding out they ran out of cake—no fun.

Filing Your First Tax Return

Filing your first tax return can feel like a rite of passage into adulthood. You'll need critical documents: your Social Security number, any forms from jobs (like a W-2 or 1099), and maybe information on student loans or your savings account interest. You can file online or on paper but online is usually faster and easier, with step-by-step software like a tax pro whispering over your shoulder.

Speaking of software, there are many options for online tax prep, from free versions for simple returns to more complex ones that cost a bit but offer extra guidance and tools. These can be a significant investment, especially if your financial situation is more "complicated adulting" than "basic adulting." Consider using TurboTax or H&R Block tax software.

Adjusting Your Tax Withholding

Have you ever gotten a considerable tax refund and felt like you won the lottery? It's fantastic, but it also means you've been giving the government an interest-free loan all year. Adjusting your withholding on your W-4 form tells your employer how much tax to take out of your paycheck. Get it just right, and you'll keep more money in your pocket all year, smoothing out your cash flow and maybe even saving you from a ramen-only diet at the end of the month.

So, as you step into the world of young adulthood, taxes don't have to be something that triggers a cold sweat. With these basics under your belt, you're well on your way to handling your taxes like an adult—intelligent, informed, and maybe even a little excited about filing your tax return. Who knew adulting could feel so good?

7.2 TAX DEDUCTIONS AND CREDITS: WHAT YOU CAN CLAIM

Navigating the tax season can feel like deciding what to binge-watch next—overwhelming, with many options. But, just like finally hitting play on a five-star series, getting a grip on tax deductions and credits can be seriously rewarding. Understanding these can be the difference between a good and a significant refund, or even owing less if you're not expecting a refund. So, let's decode the sometimes cryptic language of tax deductions and credits, ensuring you don't miss out on money-saving opportunities.

Distinguishing Between Deductions and Credits

First, let's clarify what tax deductions and credits are and how they differ. Imagine you're at a fancy restaurant; tax deductions lower the amount of your income that's subject to tax—it's like reducing the cost of your meal so the sales tax you pay is less. On the other hand, tax credits are like having a gift card; they provide a dollar-for-dollar reduction on the amount of tax you owe. So, if you owe $1,000 and have a $200 tax credit, you now owe $800. Credits can be refundable or non-refundable, which means they either reduce your tax to zero or refund you if they exceed your tax liability.

Essential Deductions for Young Adults

Every penny saved counts for many young adults, especially those fresh out of college or just starting their careers. That's where knowing your deductions comes in handy. Student loan interest deduction is a biggie. If you're paying back college loans, you can deduct up to $2,500 of the interest paid during the year. This deduction is especially valuable because you can claim it even if you don't itemize deductions on your tax return.

Remember about work-related expenses. If you're freelancing or self-employed, you can deduct business expenses like your home office, travel costs, and utilities or internet charges. However, the Tax Cuts and Jobs Act suspended unreimbursed employee expense deductions for those employed by companies, so keep that in mind.

Tax Credits That Can Be a Game Changer

Moving on to tax credits, which are often more beneficial than deductions since they reduce your tax bill directly. The American Opportunity Tax Credit (AOTC) is perfect for students currently in school. This gem offers up to $2,500 per year for things like tuition, books, and other supplies during the first four years of higher education. If the credit brings your tax you owe to zero, you can have 40% of any remaining amount of the credit (up to $1,000) refunded to you.

The Lifetime Learning Credit (LLC) is another educational credit, but it's broader. It offers up to $2,000 per tax return (not per student) and isn't limited to the first four years of college, covering graduate and professional degree courses. Then there's the Earned Income Tax Credit (EITC), designed to benefit working people with low to moderate income. The amount varies based on your income, filing status, and how many children you have, but it can substantially boost your tax situation or refund.

Maximizing Your Tax Benefits

Keeping meticulous records is crucial to make the most of these deductions and credits. Save those receipts, log your expenses as they happen, and organize your financial documents. If you need help determining whether to itemize deductions or take the standard deduction, do the math to see which saves you more money. Generally, itemizing is the way to go if your itemized deductions are more than your standard deduction. However, with increased standard deductions under recent tax law changes, many find that standard deduction is the better choice.

Navigating deductions and credits can be a smooth process. With some knowledge and organization, you can shave a significant amount off your tax bill—or, better yet, increase your refund. So, gather those documents, track those expenses, and make this tax season less stressful and more about savings. Remember, every deduction and credit you claim is like putting money back in your pocket, and who doesn't love the sound of that?

7.3 FREELANCING AND TAXES: KEEPING IT STRAIGHT

So, you've decided to dive into the freelancing pool – welcome to the deep end, where the waters are just as rewarding as they are challenging! Managing your taxes is one of the first things you'll need to get your head around. Unlike a regular 9-to-5 gig, where your employer typically handles taxes, freelancing means you're the boss, including being your tax department. Let's untangle the web of self-employment tax, quarterly payments, and all that jazz, turning you into a savvy freelance tax navigator.

Self-Employment Tax: Why You Pay Both Sides

When you're a freelancer, you're subject to self-employment tax, which covers Social Security and Medicare taxes. Usually, these are split between you and your employer, but guess what? As a freelancer, you are the employer and the employee, so you're on the hook for both halves. This might sound like a tough deal, but here's the kicker: it contributes to your future benefits, such as Social Security and Medicare, when you retire. Think of it as paying into your future self's peace of mind.

The self-employment tax rate is 15.3%, broken down into 12.4% for Social Security on the first $168,600 of your net earnings and 2.9% for Medicare with no limit. If your net earnings exceed $200,000 you are subject to an additional medicare tax of 0.9%. Yes, it adds up, but remember, this also means you're clocking in credits toward your Social Security benefits, which can be a big deal when you hit your golden years.

Quarterly Tax Payments: The Freelancer's Rhythm

When you switch from employee to freelancer, one change is the shift from annual or bi-annual tax interactions to making quarterly tax payments. Here's the deal: the IRS likes its money in regular installments throughout the year, and when you're freelancing, it's on you to make sure they get it. If you expect to owe at least $1,000 in taxes for the year, you should make quarterly estimated tax payments.

These payments are due in April, June, September, and January. Missing these dates can lead to penalties, like late fees on a forgotten bill. You must estimate your annual earnings and calculate the taxes to determine how much to pay. It sounds daunting, but it becomes another part of your business rhythm once you get the hang of it.

Tools for Tracking: Your Financial Dashboard

Keeping track of income and expenses can be the bane of a freelancer's existence, but thankfully, there's a slew of apps and software designed to make this easier. Tools like QuickBooks Soloprenuer or FreshBooks offer tailored solutions for freelancers. They can track your income, categorize expenses, and even help estimate your quarterly taxes. Think of these tools as your dashboard; they give you a clear view of your financial speed, fuel, and navigation, ensuring you don't veer off your fiscal path.

These platforms often come with handy features like receipt capture and mileage tracking, which are golden when claiming deductions. They keep your financial records tidy and audit-ready, which can be a lifesaver if the IRS ever comes knocking.

When to Call in the Pros: Hiring a Tax Professional

While apps and software can handle much of the heavy lifting, there are times when a human touch is necessary. If your tax situation is complex—maybe you've got multiple income streams, you're dabbling in international freelancing, or you're just overwhelmed—it might be wise to consult a tax professional. They can offer personalized advice, help optimize your tax returns, and guide you on tricky issues like deductions and credits specifically beneficial to freelancers.

A good tax pro can be worth their weight in gold, saving you money and the time and stress of navigating the tax labyrinth alone. Plus, they stay updated on all the latest tax changes, which means they can proactively manage your taxes, ensuring you take advantage of every possible benefit while staying compliant with the IRS.

Navigating the freelance tax world is like learning a new dance. It might step on your toes a few times, but with the right rhythm, tools, and occasionally a professional dance partner, you'll be moving to the beat of financial success in no time. Keep these insights in your back pocket, stay organized, and watch as what once seemed like a chore transforms into another part of your thriving freelance life.

7.4 INVESTMENT TAXES: WHAT YOU NEED TO KNOW

Let's dive into the sometimes thrilling, often puzzling world of investment taxes. If you've ever felt like investment taxes are a beast of their own, you're not alone. But don't worry, I'm here to arm you with the knowledge to tame this wild creature. Understanding how your investment gains and losses affect your taxes can pay off, whether you're day trading from your dorm room or investing in your first real estate.

Capital Gains and Losses: The Short and Long of It

So, here's the scoop on capital gains and losses. You make a capital gain when you sell an investment for more than you paid for it. Sell it for less, and you've got a capital loss. Simple, right? But here's where it gets interesting: the tax rate on these gains or losses depends on how long you've held the investment and held it for less than a year. That's a short-term capital gain taxed at your regular income tax rate. But suppose you hold onto your investments for over a year before selling. In that case, any gain becomes a long-term capital gain, which benefits from a lower tax rate, typically 0%, 15%, or 20%, depending on your income level.

Think of those capital losses as a financial silver lining when an investment doesn't pan out. You can use losses to offset gains. For example, if you made a $1,000 gain from selling one stock but lost $500 on another, you can subtract the loss from the gain, leaving you with a taxable gain of $500. What if your losses exceed your gains? You can use up to $3,000 of excess loss to reduce your other taxable income, giving your finances a little cushion and carry over the excess loss to the next tax year.

Specific Tax Rules for Common Investments

Each type of investment, be it stocks, bonds, mutual funds, or real estate, has its own tax rules. Stocks and mutual funds, for instance, are pretty straightforward; gains from selling them are taxed based on how long you've held them, as we discussed. Bonds, however, can get a bit trickier. Interest from most bonds is taxed as ordinary income, but exceptions exist. Take municipal bonds, for example—they often offer tax-free interest, making them a potentially attractive option for those in higher tax brackets.

Real estate investing opens up a whole new world of tax considerations. If you're flipping houses, your profits are considered regular income, taxed at your usual rate. But if you're renting out property, you must deal with depreciation, maintenance deductions, and rental income, which are also taxed as regular income. However, selling a rental property you've held for over a year qualifies for the lower long-term capital gains rate.

Dividends and Interest Income: Know Your Tax

Dividends—those pleasant little investment payouts are classified as qualified or non-qualified. Qualified dividends are taxed at the lower capital gains tax rate, which is excellent. Non-qualified dividends, however, are taxed at the higher ordinary income tax rate. Knowing which type of dividends your investments give you can help you plan your tax strategy more effectively.

Interest income from investments, like savings accounts or CDs, is taxed as ordinary income. Reporting this correctly is essential to avoid any surprises come tax time. Keep records of the interest you earn from all your investment sources throughout the year.

The Beauty of Tax-Advantaged Accounts

Now for some excellent news—tax-advantaged accounts, such as traditional IRAs, Roth IRAs, and 401(k)s, are like the superheroes of the investment world. These accounts allow your investments to grow either tax-free or tax-deferred. With a traditional IRA or 401(k), you make contributions with pre-tax dollars, and you only pay taxes when you withdraw the money, ideally in retirement when your tax rate might be lower. Roth IRAs work a bit differently; you contribute after-tax dollars, but your withdrawals in retirement are tax-free.

These accounts are powerful tools for managing both your investments and your taxes. Understanding and utilizing them can significantly enhance your financial portfolio's efficiency and future economic stability. Remember, the earlier you start contributing to these accounts, the more your money can grow, thanks to the magic of compounding returns. So, dive into your investment strategies with these tax tips, and make the most of your financial adventures!

7.5 SALARY NEGOTIATION TACTICS FOR YOUR FIRST JOB

Let's talk business—or, in this case, talk money. Salary negotiation is that nail-biting stage of the job interview process where you've got to strap on your armor and fight for your worth. Yep, it's not just about getting the job; it's about getting paid what you deserve. And trust me, getting this right can set the tone for your career. Here's why: every salary negotiation sets a precedent for future earnings. It's like setting the starting line in a race—the better your start, the better your position in the long run. That bump in salary doesn't just affect your paycheck now; it compounds over time, influencing raises, bonuses, and even future job offers. Plus, it's a chance to show your new employer that you understand your value and are not afraid to advocate for yourself—a skill that's golden in any career.

So, how do you survive your first salary negotiation and nail it? First up, preparation is critical. I'd like you to dive into research mode and determine the going rate for your position in the industry and geographic area. Websites like Glassdoor can be your best friends here. Knowing these numbers isn't just about setting expectations but backing up your request with cold, complex data. It's much harder for an employer to lowball you if you can diplomatically say, "According to my research…"

Now, let's talk strategy. Before you even get to the negotiation table, have a clear idea of your ideal salary and the minimum you're willing to accept. These are your "wish" and your "walk" numbers. This range gives you negotiation wiggle room and ensures you won't be caught off guard if they flip the script and ask you what salary you want.

Handling the Negotiation Dance

Picture this: you're in the room, and the moment has arrived to talk numbers. The employer throws out the first offer. Now, play it cool even if that number has you secretly doing a happy dance inside because it's more than you expected. It's standard practice to make a counteroffer. Express genuine appreciation for the offer, then lay down your well-researched counteroffer. A good rule of thumb? Aim about 10-15% higher than their offer, giving you room to meet in the middle. Remember, this is a dance, not a duel. Keep the tone positive and professional, showing that you're looking for a fair deal and reflecting your worth and excitement about the opportunity.

But what if they play hardball or claim that the budget won't budge? That's your cue to pivot to non-salary benefits. Maybe it's a bump in vacation days, the flexibility to work from home a couple of days a week, or opportunities for professional development and training that can boost your career. Perks like these can sometimes be just as valuable as a higher salary. They can improve your work-life balance, enhance job satisfaction, and contribute to professional growth.

Negotiating your salary is like a chess game. Each move should be thoughtful and strategic, pushing towards an endgame where both parties feel like winners. Keep your wits about you, don't be afraid to ask for what you deserve, and always be ready to highlight how your skills and experiences are an asset to the company. With the proper preparation and mindset, you'll walk away with a better offer and the confidence from knowing how to advocate for yourself. And that, my friends, is worth its weight in gold.

7.6 PASSIVE INCOME: MAKING MONEY WHILE YOU SLEEP

Imagine earning money while binge-watching your favorite series or sleeping on a lazy Sunday afternoon. Sounds pretty sweet, right? That's the beauty of passive income—making money without actively working. It's like having a magical money tree in your backyard, except it's real and achievable with the right strategies.

Understanding Passive Income and Its Perks

Passive income is your financial buddy that keeps giving without the constant effort on your part. Unlike active income, which you earn from a job or freelancing, passive income streams generate earnings regularly from investments or assets you've set up once. Think of it as setting a series of dominos in motion; you do the work upfront to line them up meticulously, and then, with a single flick, they continue to topple without needing your help to push each one individually.

This type of income is more about 'income continuity' rather than 'instant gratification.' It ensures a flow of cash even when you're not clocking in hours, providing a cushion that can help cover expenses, boost savings, or fund that dream vacation. Moreover, it's a key component in building wealth and financial security over time, giving you a taste of economic freedom that allows you to choose what you want to do with your time.

Famous Passive Income Avenues for Young Adults

Now, let's dive into some of the most accessible passive income ideas for you. Real estate investments are a classic choice. Purchasing a property and renting it out can provide a steady monthly income. With platforms like Airbnb, you can even rent out part of your home or your entire place for short periods at potentially higher rates than traditional leasing.

Next up, dividend stocks. These are shares of companies that pay you a portion of their earnings regularly. It's like being a silent partner in a business where you reap benefits without attending board meetings or managing day-to-day operations. Investing in a diversified portfolio of dividend-paying stocks can create a stream of income with the added potential for capital gains.

Do you have a knack for writing or a particular expertise? Consider writing a book or creating an online course. Once you've put in the initial effort to develop and publish your work, it can continue to sell without much additional input. Platforms like Amazon for eBooks or Udemy for courses make it easier to reach a global audience and earn royalties or course fees.

The Real Deal: Effort and Investment Needed

It's crucial to note that while passive income streams may eventually require little effort, they often need significant upfront investment or work. For instance, buying a property usually requires a down payment and a mortgage, not to mention the time and money spent on maintenance and management. Similarly, building a portfolio of dividend stocks requires an initial financial outlay and some savvy investing knowledge to choose the right stocks.

Even seemingly simple projects like writing a book involve hours of writing, editing, and marketing before you can see any real income. The key is to approach passive income with a realistic mindset. Understand that the initial phase is often the most demanding, requiring time and money to set things up.

Success Stories That Inspire

Let's look at some real-life examples. Take Clara, who bought a small apartment in a tourist-friendly city. After setting it up for short-term rentals, she now earns enough to cover her mortgage and living expenses without working full-time. Then there's Raj, who invested in dividend stocks throughout his 20s. By the time he hit 30, his investments were yielding enough annually to fund his master's degree without dipping into his savings.

These stories underline that while establishing a passive income can be intensive, the financial and personal freedom it offers can be life-changing. By choosing the right passive income strategies that align with your financial goals and lifestyle, you can set up a future where your money works for you, giving you the freedom to live on your terms.

As we wrap up this exploration of passive income, remember that it's part of a larger financial picture. While setting up passive income streams, manage your expenses, invest wisely, and stay financially informed. Next, we'll delve deeper into intelligent financial habits that can help you build and maintain wealth. So stay tuned, take action, and watch your passive income streams flourish, bolstering your financial journey.

CHAPTER 8
BUILDING FINANCIAL INDEPENDENCE AND SECURITY

So, you've decided to get serious about your finances, huh? Consider this chapter your wise, slightly quirky guide to navigating the financial milestones in your 20s and 30s. It's like leveling up in a video game where the rewards are real money and financial peace of mind—pretty sweet, right? From tackling student loans to saving for a shiny new home or even starting a family, we'll map out the key milestones you should aim for and precisely how to hit each one. Ready to get your financial game face on? Let's do this!

8.1 FINANCIAL MILESTONES FOR YOUR 20S AND 30S

Identify Key Financial Milestones

Navigating your 20s and 30s can sometimes feel like a contestant on a game show—complete with exciting prizes and perplexing challenges. Key financial milestones are your game levels, and boy, do they make life enjoyable! First, there's the *Student Loan Boss Fight*, where you strategize to knock out those pesky loans. Winning this battle requires a solid payment plan and some clever refinancing moves.

Next, you're saving for a down payment on a home, like gathering coins in a platformer game—every little bit gets you closer to that big purchase. And hey, if starting a family is on your horizon, you need a whole new budget line for baby gear, daycare, and, eventually, a college fund. Each of these milestones isn't just a financial goal; they're stepping stones to your next life stage, and boy, does it feel good to reach them.

Set Realistic and Achievable Goals

Setting goals is all great, but if they're not SMART (Specific, Measurable, Achievable, Relevant, Time-bound), they might as well be wishes tossed into a fountain. Start by being super specific. Instead of saying, "I want to save money," aim for, "I want to save $10,000 for a home down payment in two years." See the difference? It's like the difference between saying, "I want to get fit," versus "I want to run a 5K in under 30 minutes by December." One gives you a clear target and timeframe, making pulling out your financial sneakers and getting to work much easier.

Encourage Regular Financial Check-Ins

Life's always throwing us curveballs, right? Maybe you get a job promotion (woohoo!), or a surprise expense pops up (ouch). That's why it's crucial to have regular financial check-ins. Think of these like your regular tune-ups for your car; they keep everything running smoothly. Every few months, sit down with a cup of your favorite brew, review your budget, progress towards your goals, and adjust as needed. It's about steering your financial ship with intention and ensuring you're still on course for all those dreams and goals.

Provide Tools for Tracking Progress

Keeping track of all these financial details can be easier than remembering where you left your keys. But thanks to technology, there are some fantastic tools out there to help keep you on track. Apps like Rocket Money or YNAB (You Need A Budget) can be lifesavers. They allow you to track your spending, set up budget categories, and even send you cheerful (or stern, depending on your settings) reminders about your goals. It's like having a personal financial coach in your pocket, cheering you on as you sprint towards your financial fitness peaks.

So, as you lace up your financial boots and set out to conquer these milestones, remember that each step you take builds your confidence and gets you closer to the ultimate prize of economic independence. Please keep your eyes on the prize and your hands on the budget, and let's crush these goals together!

8.2 LONG-TERM FINANCIAL PLANNING: LOOKING AHEAD

Let's talk about long-term financial planning, like planning an epic road trip across the country. You'll need a map, some good tunes, and a solid plan for pit stops (and maybe a few snacks). But instead of roadside attractions, we're focusing on the biggies: retirement, investments, savings, and those sneaky healthcare costs that can pop up. Think of long-term financial planning as your GPS for navigating life's financial highways. It's about setting up a plan that covers your bases now and down the road, ensuring smoother rides and fewer bumps.

Now, could you tell me why this is so important? Without a roadmap, it's easy to take wrong turns and end up somewhere you didn't intend—like realizing you're set to retire, but your bank account didn't get the memo. Starting early with a retirement savings plan, diversified investments, and a cushion for healthcare expenses can prepare you for a comfy financial future. And let's be honest, who doesn't want to retire with enough cash to start that alpaca farm or travel the world finally?

Strategies for Risk Management

When managing financial risks, it's all about not putting all your eggs in one basket—or, in finance speak, diversification. This means spreading your investments across different assets like stocks, bonds, and real estate, so if one market dips, you're not reeling from total disaster. It's like weatherproofing your financial house, ensuring a storm in one part doesn't wreck the whole structure.

Setting up contingency funds is another crucial strategy. This is your financial safety net, ready to catch you if a job loss, medical emergency, or unexpected roof repair (because it always happens during a rainstorm, right?) throws you for a loop. This fund isn't just about covering costs; it's about peace of mind. And let's be honest: Are you sleeping better at night knowing you're covered? That's worth its weight in gold.

Guide on Retirement Planning

Alright, onto retirement planning. If you think it's too early to consider retirement, think again. The earlier you start, the more you benefit from compound interest—basically, the interest on your investments earns interest, which adds up big time over the years. So, how much should you be saving? A good rule of thumb is to stash away at least 15% of your income annually for retirement. It sounds like a chunk, but remember, this is your future self we're talking about. Treat them kindly.

As for where to stash that cash, look into retirement accounts like 401(k)s, especially if your employer offers a match (free money, people!). Traditional and Roth IRAs are also fantastic options with tax advantages. Choosing the suitable investment options within these accounts—like mutual funds, bonds, or stocks—depends on your time horizon and risk tolerance. It's like choosing the right gear for a hike; you want to ensure it fits your needs and the terrain.

Proactive Approach to Financial Wellness

Finally, a proactive approach to your financial health can make all the difference. This means regularly educating yourself about financial matters, staying on top of market changes, and maybe even working with a financial advisor if things get too complex. Think of them as your financial fitness coach, helping you stay agile and informed.

So, dive into these strategies, tweak them as your life evolves, and keep your eyes on the prize—a financially secure future where you call the shots. Remember, long-term planning isn't just about money; it's about crafting the life you want, to retirement and beyond. So, let's get planning, stay proactive, and make sure your financial map is guiding you exactly where you want to go. Keep up the excellent work, and here's to a future that's as bright as your best-laid financial plans!

8.3 INSURANCE: TYPES, NEEDS, AND DECISIONS

Let's crack open the not-so-mysterious world of insurance because, let's face it, not knowing your way around it can be like trying to play a video game without knowing the controls – frustrating and likely to end in disaster. Insurance, in all its forms, is essentially your financial safety net. That trusty sidekick steps in to save the day when things go south, whether it's a fender bender or a medical hiccup. So, let's break down the essential types and get you savvy about covering your assets!

Navigating the Insurance Landscape

First off, health insurance is your frontline defense. Without it, a simple trip to the ER can morph into a financial nightmare faster than you can say "stitches." It's not just about emergencies; regular check-ups, prescriptions, and preventive care are all part of keeping you in tip-top shape without the hefty price tags.

Then there's life insurance, the unsung hero for those with loved ones relying on their financial support. Consider it your legacy, ensuring your family can maintain their lifestyle, even if you're not around. It's not the cheeriest thing to think about, but it's a crucial piece of the puzzle for peace of mind.

Moving on to auto insurance—unless you plan to wrap your car in bubble wrap, you will need a solid policy. It's not just about repairs; it's also about protecting yourself against liability if you're ever at fault in an accident. And trust me, saying "sorry" doesn't entirely cover the costs if you rear-end someone's brand-new ride.

Securing your castle (or cozy apartment) is critical for homeowners and renters. Homeowner's insurance doesn't just cover repairs; it protects you from theft, natural disasters, and even the odd lawsuit if someone decides to sue after slipping on your front steps. Renter's insurance, while often overlooked, offers a safety net for your belongings and can cover unexpected damages because sometimes life—and leaky ceilings—happen.

Choosing the Right Coverage

Now, choosing the right insurance isn't just choosing the cheapest option. It's like picking a meal at a restaurant; the most affordable dish might save you a few bucks, but will it satisfy you? Start by assessing your needs. If you're a globe-trotting adventurer, you'll want a health plan that covers international mishaps. Drive a luxury car? Better get coverage that matches its pedigree.

Please take a look at how much coverage you need. It's a balancing act between not overpaying for excessive coverage and not skimping to the point of peril. For instance, life insurance could be multiple times your annual income to ensure your family's comfort.

In contrast, your auto insurance should at least cover the total value of your assets for liability so a lawsuit doesn't wipe you out.

The Perils of Underinsurance

Being underinsured is like wearing a raincoat that stops at your elbows; it might provide some protection, but you'll still get soaked. Underinsured homeowners can face significant out-of-pocket costs for repairs after a calamity. And if you're relying on minimum auto insurance, a severe accident could see your savings evaporate faster than water on a hot engine. The repercussions can ripple out, derailing financial plans and putting long-term goals on hold. It's a risky game that can cost you more than just money—it can cost peace of mind.

Hunting for the Best Insurance Deals

Finally, let's talk shopping for insurance because who doesn't love a good deal? Start by comparing policies like you compare smartphones—look beyond the price tag. Check out deductibles, coverage limits, and exclusions. It's about finding the sweet spot where cost and coverage meet your needs perfectly.

Don't shy away from using an insurance broker. These folks are like personal shoppers for your insurance; they do the legwork, compare offers, and can often snag discounts you didn't even know existed. Plus, they can explain the fine print in plain English, saving you from the head-scratching terms that can leave you more baffled than enlightened.

So, gear up with the right insurance, and you'll safeguard your wallet and gain the freedom to live your life with one less worry hanging over your head. Whether sailing the high seas or navigating daily commutes, the right coverage ensures you're ready for anything life throws your way, keeping your financial goals intact and on track. Now, with your insurance game strong, you can focus on what matters – living your best life and being secure in knowing you're well protected.

8.4 ESTATE PLANNING BASICS FOR YOUNG ADULTS

Let's be honest: talking about estate planning can feel like bringing up flossing at a party—necessary, but not exactly fun. However, like flossing, the sooner you tackle estate planning, the better off you'll be. So, what is estate planning, and why should someone just starting to make their mark in the world care about it? Well, it's making sure that your assets (yeah, even that old car and your laptop) and health decisions are handled the way you want if you can't make those calls yourself due to illness or—if we're being sincere—death.

I know what you're thinking: "But I'm young and hardly have any assets. Why would I need estate planning?" Here's the thing—it's not just about who gets your comic book collection; it's also about making sure you have a say in your health care and financial decisions if you end up incapacitated because you tried a double backflip on your snowboard. It's about protecting yourself and your stuff and making things easier for your family if they need to step in.

Critical Components of a Basic Estate Plan

First up, let's talk about wills and living trusts. Having a will is like having a detailed instruction manual for your loved ones on handling your things after you're gone. It tells everyone what you want to happen, which can prevent a lot of family disagreements and legal headaches. On the other hand, a living trust is like allowing someone to manage your assets if you can't do it yourself without court intervention. It's a bit more complex than a will but can provide more control and privacy over handling your assets.

Next, there's the durable power of attorney. This document lets you appoint someone you trust to manage your financial affairs if you can't. Think of it as handing over your financial video game controller when you can't play anymore. Then there's the healthcare directive, or living will, which lets you specify what kind of medical treatment you do or don't want if you can't speak for yourself. It's like ensuring your health care follows a script you've written in advance.

How to Start Estate Planning

So, how do you think you could get this all sorted? First, take a deep breath. It's more manageable than it sounds. Start by taking stock of what you have: your assets, debts, and anything else that might need to be dealt with if you're unable to manage them yourself. Then, think about your wishes for those assets and your health care. Who do you trust to handle your finances or make medical decisions? These are big questions, but answering them now can save a lot of stress later.

The next step is finding a good estate planning attorney. There are better times to DIY with online forms; getting professional advice is crucial. Could you look for someone with experience who listens to your concerns and speaks in plain English rather than legalese? They can help you draft a will, set up a trust, and get all those other documents in order.

Debunking Common Misconceptions

Let's bust some myths while we're at it. First, estate planning isn't just for the rich. No matter how much or how little you own, you have an estate and can benefit from planning how it's handled. And you're never too young to start. Life is unpredictable, and having a plan is just brilliant, not morbid. It's about taking control of your future, no matter what happens.

Estate planning might seem like something you can put off until you're older, but it's about giving yourself peace of mind now. It's ensuring that whatever you've worked hard for is protected and that your wishes are followed, no matter what. So, don't wait. Start thinking about your estate plan today, and take the first steps towards securing you and your family's future. It's one of the most responsible things you can do—and hey, it'll give you one less thing to worry about as you go back to planning that next snowboarding trick or whatever adventure you've got lined up next.

8.5 ACHIEVING FINANCIAL FREEDOM: REAL STORIES, REAL ADVICE

Let's demystify this whole concept of financial freedom. It's not about swimming in a vault of gold coins like some cartoon billionaire; it's about reaching a point where financial constraints no longer tie you down. Imagine making life choices without money worries nipping at your heels—switching careers, taking a sabbatical to travel, or working less to spend more time on hobbies or with family. That's financial freedom: the ultimate level-up in the game of life where money is no longer the boss of your choices.

Now, let me share some stories of folks who've cracked the code on financial independence. Take Leo, for instance. He started in a typical nine-to-five, but he began freelancing with a passion for graphic design. Fast forward a few years, and his side gig exploded into a full-fledged design studio. By diversifying his income streams and balancing client work with passive income from digital assets like templates and tutorials, Leo can now pick projects that excite him without stress about the price tag.

Then there's Jenna, who made it her mission to live mortgage-free. She and her partner opted to live in a smaller, more affordable home, aggressively paying their mortgage early in their careers. Now in their late 30s, they own their home outright and enjoy the financial breathing room from having no housing payments. Jenna's story is a powerful reminder of how traditional saving and investing can pave the way to economic liberty.

Exploring Passive Income as a Freedom Tool

Passive income is like the secret sauce to financial independence. Money keeps coming in without you having to grind day in and day out. Think of it as setting up a series of money-making machines that do the work for you. For example, an avid photographer, Sarah, started selling her photos on stock image websites. What began as a hobby now brings in steady monthly checks covering her groceries and utility bills, allowing her to invest more time in creative projects without financial strain.

Another champ of passive income is Tom, who bought a duplex as a young adult. He lives in one unit and rents out the other, which covers his mortgage and maintenance costs. This setup cuts down his living expenses and builds equity in a property that will likely appreciate over time. It's an intelligent move that positions him for greater financial security.

Actionable Advice for Your Financial Freedom Quest

Alright, ready to start your journey toward financial freedom? Here's some actionable advice to get you rolling. First, zero in on reducing high-interest debt. Those interest charges can eat up your income faster than you can say "bankruptcy." Consider methods like the debt avalanche, where you pay off debts from the highest interest rate to the lowest. This strategy saves you money in the long run and frees up more cash for saving and investing.

Next, embrace budgeting. Yeah, it sounds about as fun as watching paint dry, but knowing where your money goes each month is crucial. Use apps like Rocket Money or PocketGuard to track your spending patterns and identify areas where you can cut back without sacrificing your joy. The goal here is to create a budget that reflects your values and priorities, giving you a clear path to saving more aggressively.

Don't forget to invest in yourself. Enhancing your skills can lead to better job opportunities, higher income, and more freedom. Whether taking courses, attending workshops, or just reading up on your industry, staying competitive is critical. Also, consider investing in the stock market or real estate to grow your wealth. Remember, the more assets you generate income from, the closer you are to financial freedom.

So, as you embark on this adventure, keep these stories and tips in mind. They're not just tales of success; they're blueprints that show what's possible when you approach your finances with intention and creativity. Whether you're dreaming of a life of travel, entrepreneurship, or simply more time with loved ones, financial freedom is a decisive step toward making those dreams a reality.

8.6 KEEPING UP WITH FINANCIAL TRENDS: STAYING INFORMED

Staying current with financial trends is akin to updating your smartphone apps—you ensure you always use the best version available for optimum performance. In the whirlwind world of finance, what you know today might not hold tomorrow, and that's why keeping a pulse on the economic landscape can drastically sway your financial strategies in the right direction. Think of it as your financial newsfeed, consistently refreshing to bring the most relevant and beneficial information to your fingertips.

Why is this so crucial, you might ask? Financial markets are as dynamic as a season finale of your favorite series—always throwing curveballs. By staying informed, you can make numerous decisions that align with current economic conditions, meaning better investment choices, more brilliant saving strategies, and a more robust understanding of the global economy. It's all about turning this knowledge into a tool to navigate through your personal financial goals more efficiently and with more flair.

Now, diving into the sea of financial news might seem daunting, but it's all about knowing where to cast your net. Start with trusted financial news outlets that have been around the block, like The Wall Street Journal, Bloomberg, and CNBC. These platforms are the big fish in the sea, providing a broad view of financial markets, economic reports, and personal finance trends. For the tech-savvy, financial blogs like The Financial Diet or podcasts such as "Planet Money" make understanding complex economic concepts as easy as streaming a playlist. They break down intricate topics into digestible pieces, often adding a pinch of humor to keep you engaged.

But don't stop there! Engaging with financial communities can amplify your understanding and introduce you to perspectives you might not have considered. Online forums like Reddit's r/personalfinance or financial subgroups on platforms like LinkedIn offer a treasure trove of real-life advice, experiences, and strategies shared by individuals from all walks of economic life. Attending seminars and workshops, even virtually, can also be a game-changer. These gatherings are not just about listening; they're interactive, allowing you to ask questions, debate concepts, and network with others just as eager to master their financial destinies.

Applying what you learn to your financial planning is where the magic happens. It's like customizing your character in a game; you tailor your financial strategies based on the latest, most relevant information you've gathered. For instance, if you learn about a rising trend in tech stocks through a podcast, you can consider how investing in that sector might fit into your broader investment strategy. Or, if a blog post discusses the latest in robo-advisors, you might decide to try one out to optimize your investments. The key is to always weigh this information against your personal financial goals and circumstances—what works for one person's portfolio might not make sense for yours.

SUMMARIZING FINANCIAL SAVVY

Wrapping up and keeping your finger on the pulse of financial trends isn't just about accumulating knowledge; it's about transforming that knowledge into actionable insights that propel your personal finance goals forward. From selecting credible sources and joining vibrant financial communities to practically applying newfound wisdom, every step equips you with the tools to navigate the ever-changing financial waters confidently. As we pivot from understanding trends to exploring deeper investment strategies in the next chapter, remember that the goal is to witness economic growth and actively participate in shaping it. Let's continue to turn insights into actions as we forge ahead to more advanced financial maneuvers.

Keeping the Game Alive

Now that you have everything you need to achieve, it's time to pass on your new knowledge and show other readers where they can get the same help.

Leaving your honest opinion of this book on Amazon will show other young adults where they can find the information. They're looking for a way to achieve financial confidence, reduce debt, invest wisely, and pass their passion for personal finance from young adults to young adults forward.

I appreciate your help. Personal finance for young adults is kept alive when we pass on our knowledge, and you're helping us to do just that.

Scan the QR code or visit the link below to leave your review:

https://www.amazon.com/review/review-your-purchases/?asin=B0DBM14Y9H

REFERENCES

- The Best Budget Apps for 2024 <https://www.nerdwallet.com/article/finance/best-budget-apps>
- How to Improve Your Credit Score Fast <https://www.experian.com/blogs/ask-experian/credit-education/improving-credit/improve-credit-score/>
- 6 Steps to Creating an Emergency Fund - Morgan Stanley <https://www.morganstanley.com/articles/how-to-build-an-emergency-fund>
- Understanding employment taxes | Internal Revenue Service <https://www.irs.gov/businesses/small-businesses-self-employed/understanding-employment-taxes>
- How Your Impulse Spending Is Hurting Your Finances <https://finance.yahoo.com/news/impulse-spending-hurting-finances-161159415.html>
- Overwhelmed by subscriptions? Here are eight tips to save ... <https://www.washingtonpost.com/technology/2023/06/22/organize-subscriptions/>
- 7 Credit Card Tips For Beginners <https://www.bankrate.com/credit-cards/building-credit/credit-card-tips-for-new-users/>
- The Biden-Harris Administration's Student Debt Relief Plan ... <https://studentaid.gov/debt-relief-announcement>
- How to Lower Your Credit Card Interest Rate <https://www.investopedia.com/articles/pf/08/negotiate-credit-card-apr.asp>
- Predatory Lending: How to Avoid, Examples and Protections <https://www.investopedia.com/terms/p/predatory_lending.asp>
- The Best Investments for Young Adults <https://www.investopedia.com/articles/younginvestors/12/best-investments-for-young-people.asp>
- The Link Between Compound Interest and Your Retirement ... <https://plattwealthmanagement.com/compound-interest-and-your-retirement-contributions/>
- Cryptocurrency Explained With Pros and Cons for Investment <https://www.investopedia.com/terms/c/cryptocurrency.asp>
- Real Estate Investing for Beginners — A Guide to Getting Started <https://equitymultiple.com/blog/real-estate-investing-for-beginners>
- 4 Types of Insurance Policies and Coverage You Need <https://www.

REFERENCES

- investopedia.com/financial-edge/0212/4-types-of-insurance-everyone-needs.aspx>
- How to start preparing for retirement in your 20s <https://www.cnbc.com/2023/12/07/how-to-start-preparing-for-retirement-in-your-20s.html>
- Financial Planning for Major Life Events: From Marriage to ... <https://www.fool.com/investing/2023/06/01/financial-planning-for-major-life-events-from-marr/>
- Top 5 Finance Automation Tools for 2024: Streamline Your ... <https://www.solvexia.com/blog/financial-automation-software-top-tools>
- Budgeting Strategies: 50/30/20 vs. Zero-Based <https://thecollegeinvestor.com/17638/budgeting-for-your-personality/>
- Proactive Steps for Ensuring Data Security in Fintech App ... <https://medium.com/appfoster/proactive-steps-for-ensuring-data-security-in-fintech-app-development-68f1349449d>
- How to Create Multiple Streams of Income <https://www.cnb.com/personal-banking/insights/create-multiple-streams-of-income.html>
- How to Budget After a Job Loss <https://www.ramseysolutions.com/budgeting/budgeting-after-job-loss>
- How to Negotiate Medical Bills: A Step-By-Step Guide <https://www.thesuperbill.com/blog/how-to-negotiate-medical-bills-a-step-by-step-guide>
- Breaking The Paycheck-To-Paycheck Cycle: 7 Steps to Financial Security <https://www.forbes.com/sites/winniesun/2023/09/07/breaking-the-paycheck-to-paycheck-cycle-7-steps-to-financial-security/>
- How to Rebuild Credit After Bankruptcy <https://www.nerdwallet.com/article/finance/rebuild-credit-after-bankruptcy>
- The 11 Stages of Wealth: Which Stage of Wealth are You at? <https://investmentmoats.com/financial-independence/stages-of-wealth-financial-independence/>
- Community Investing 101 - Investopedia <https://www.investopedia.com/articles/basics/12/community-investing.asp>
- Does Money Buy Happiness? Actually, Yes - Forbes <https://www.forbes.com/sites/johnjennings/2024/02/12/money-buys-happiness-after-all/>
- Leave a Legacy: Strategies for a Lasting Impact - U.S. Bank <https://www.usbank.com/wealth-management/financial-perspectives/trust-and-estate-planning/what-does-it-mean-to-leave-a-legacy.html>
- North Carolina Estate Planning: What You Need to Know - Plekan Law. <https://plekanlaw.com/north-carolina-estate-planning-what-you-need-to-know/>

REFERENCES

- 6 ways estate planning can save your family money - Reviewed. <https://reviewed.usatoday.com/money/features/6-ways-estate-planning-can-save-your-family-money>
- Fostering a Safer, More Secure Digital World, One Learner at a Time - Digital First Magazine. <https://www.digitalfirstmagazine.com/fostering-a-safer-more-secure-digital-world-one-learner-at-a-time/>
- Soul Number 8: All You Should Know - Ritual Meditations. <https://ritualmeditations.com/soul-number-8/>
- Free Guide - Michelle Is Your Coach. <https://michelle-is-your-coach.com/free-guide/>
- Schwarcz, S. (2022). Regulating Global Stablecoins: A Model-Law Strategy. Vanderbilt Law Review, 75(6), 1729-1785. - Vanderbilt Law Review
- Real Estate Investing for Beginners: A Guide to Neighborhood Analysis | Mashvisor. <https://www.mashvisor.com/blog/neighborhood-analysis-beginner-investors/>
- Elder Law Mishmash June 2023 - EZ Elder Law. <https://www.ezelderlaw.com/elder-law-mishmash-june-2023/>
- How to Start Preparing for Retirement in Your 20s - Thrive Global. <https://community.thriveglobal.com/how-to-start-preparing-for-retirement-in-your-20s/>
- XpenseBee® | Expense Tracker & Budget Planner. <https://www.xpensebee.com/>
- 4 Types Of Insurance Policies And Coverage You Need To Know. <https://www.newsilike.in/types-of-insurance-policies-and-coverage/>
- Strategies for Homebuyers: Navigating High Mortgage Rates Above 7%. <https://www.the812andyou.com/post/strategies-for-homebuyers-navigating-high-mortgage-rates-above-7/>
- The Ultimate Guide To Using A Business Expense Tracker Template. <https://www.pruneyardinn.com/business-expense-tracker-template/>
- How To Retire Financially Free With ONLY 1 HOUR Of Your Pay. <https://www.odettarockheadkerr.com/post/how-to-retire-financially-free-with-only-1-hour-of-your-pay>

www.ingramcontent.com/pod-product-compliance
Lightning Source LLC
Chambersburg PA
CBHW071928210526
45479CB00002B/596